Measuring
Software Reuse

Measuring Software Reuse

PRINCIPLES, PRACTICES, AND ECONOMIC MODELS

Jeffrey S. Poulin

ADDISON-WESLEY

An imprint of Addison Wesley Longman, Inc.

Reading, Massachusetts   Harlow, England   Menlo Park, California
Berkeley, California   Don Mills, Ontario   Sydney
Bonn   Amsterdam   Tokyo   Mexico City

Library of Congress Cataloging-in-Publication Data

Poulin, Jeffrey S., 1960–
    Measuring software reuse : principles, practices, and economic
  models / Jeffrey S. Poulin.
      p.   cm.
  Includes bibliographical references and index.
  ISBN 0-201-63413-9
    1. Computer software--Reusability.   I. Title.
  QA76.76.R47P68   1997
  005.1'4--dc20   96-36000
                                        CIP

The publisher offers discounts on this book when ordered in quantity for special sales.

For more information, please contact:

Corporate & Professional Publishing Group
Addison-Wesley Publishing Company
One Jacob Way
Reading, Massachusetts 01867

Text printed on recycled and acid-free paper

ISBN 0-201-63413-9
1 2 3 4 5 6 7 8 9 - MA - 99989796
First printing, November 1996

For my
grandparents.

❖

Contents

Chapter 1   *1*

MOTIVATING SOFTWARE REUSE THROUGH METRICS

Chapter 2   *9*

A REUSE METRICS OVERVIEW

Chapter 3   *21*

THE RELATIVE COSTS OF DEVELOPING WITH AND FOR REUSE

Chapter 4   33

DEFINING REUSE FROM A METRICS POINT OF VIEW

Chapter 5   61

MEASURING REUSE AND REUSE BENEFITS

Chapter 6   *91*

IMPLEMENTING A METRICS PROGRAM

Figures

Tables

❖

Foreword

Welcome to the best book on software reuse metrics available anywhere.

That's a pretty strong statement, as you might have noticed, but, as they say in Texas, "If you can't walk the walk, don't talk the talk." This book means business, and business is what reuse is all about. Reuse makes sense, dollars and cents, I like to think, and if you want to invest wisely, then the place to start is creating a business case to quantify your return on investment. As Ted Biggerstaff, the chairman of the first reuse workshop at ITT in 1983, once stated: "Reuse is like a savings account: before you can collect any interest, you have to make a deposit, and the more you put in, the greater the dividend." This book will help readers invest wisely.

Now you probably have some idea about the importance of reuse metrics, but after you are done reading this book, you will be encouraged as well as discouraged: encouraged because you will now understand the why, the what, and the how of developing and using reuse metrics; and (maybe somewhat) discouraged because you will now be aware of the discipline that needs to be applied in order for you to be successful in achieving meaningful results. While software metrics work best in stable, mature organizations, if taken seriously they can be used to raise the level of performance in any group or organization. This book is written for those who want to improve their software development process and have recognized that reuse is one of the keys.

I am glad this book was written, and I can't think of anyone more qualified to have put it together. Jeff has done a thorough job surveying, summarizing, and synthesizing a topic not for the faint of heart. Reuse is intuitively attractive, but economically it suffers from the chicken and the egg problem: "Before you can reuse software, you need software to reuse." In order to overcome negative momentum, one can set forth the following argument: The best way to bootstrap reuse is to get management to invest in the development of reusable assets. The best way to convince management to fund the development of reusable assets is to make a good business case. The best way to build a good business case is to quantify the factors associated with developing reusable software and developing applications with reusable software.

The best way to understand these factors is to read this book. If this all sounds like a sales pitch, then it probably is my alter ego, the used-program salesman, shining through. In closing, I would like to relate one of my "Confessions of a Used Program Salesman." It has to do with what I call the "Reuse Diet Plan." Basically, we can continue with our current big, slow, lethargic software development processes, or we can "slim down" by developing less. Most of us would like our business to be "lean and mean," to be in better shape to quickly react to the demands of the changing marketplace. A reuse diet is one way to get in shape, but central to this whole analogy is the concept of having a target weight to "slim down" to. If one accepts a goal—to reduce the time to market, number of errors, or production cost—then one clearly needs a way of measuring progress. In the case of any diet, a scale is important to not only capture your starting and ending weight, but to measure progress—in other words, to find out what is and what isn't working, along the way. The same is true with reuse metrics. They are important not only in setting your goal, but in gauging you progress as you travel the reuse road. Management also needs to get involved. Whether management uses a carrot or a stick to motivate their employees, they still need a yardstick to measure progress, and that is what this book is all about.

Will Tracz
Lockheed Martin Federal Systems, Mail Drop 0210, (607) 751-2169
Will.Tracz@lmco.com — 1801 State Route 17C, Owego, NY 13827-3998

❖

Preface

This book explains the most important issue in reuse measurement—defining what to count as reuse, how to count it, and *why*. Without a uniform understanding of what to count, all reports of reuse levels and benefits become automatically suspect. By addressing this issue, this book puts reuse measurement into a reliable and consistent context. Furthermore, it emphasizes a fundamental truth in software reuse:

> **Business decisions drive reuse!**

Metrics make business decisions possible by quantifying and justifying the investments necessary to make reuse happen. Metrics put into numbers the significant contribution that reuse can make to an organization's software development competitive advantage and survival. Once an organization collects the data and shows the return on investment, the business decision will support the most cost-effective way of building software!

This book aims to give the reader the background necessary to implement and understand reuse metrics. Part of this understanding includes an introduction to major metric models. However, this book adds value to the original presentations of each model by explaining each model within a common framework and by helping to explain when to apply a particular model.

In Chapter 1, "Motivating Software Reuse through Metrics," we introduce the reader to reuse and to the importance of metrics, both in a reuse program and in evaluating experience reports published by others. Chapter 2, "A Reuse Metrics Overview," serves as an introduction to the issues surrounding reuse metrics: the types of metrics, economic models, return-on-investment analysis, and cost–benefit analysis. Chapter 3, "The Relative Costs of Developing with and for Reuse," presents quantitative data on the relative benefits and costs of reuse. This data, pulled from numerous sources and experiences, establishes the foundation for many of the economic models presented in this book.

Chapter 4, "Defining Reuse from a Metrics Point of View," contains perhaps the most important material in the field of reuse metrics; it explores the issue of *what to count as reuse*. This chapter reveals how the values reported in reuse metrics can range from realistic representations of reuse activity to the extremely misleading. Chapter 5, "Measuring Reuse and Reuse Benefits," pulls all the models together by summarizing the models, discussing the strengths of each, and recommending when to apply each one.

Chapter 6, "Implementing a Metrics Program," gives a recommended set of metrics for a reuse program. The chapter gives examples of how to use the metrics, as well as an extensive case study of how to apply the metrics on a project. Along with sample worksheets given in an appendix, this chapter can help readers apply the information in this book to their own reuse programs.

From there, the book provides a discussion of different approaches to software reusability metrics. Although these approaches have been successful and innovative in identifying attributes of reusability, Chapter 7, "Measuring Software Reusability," explains why a general reusability metric will probably never exist. Nonetheless, we can use the attributes of reusability in many useful ways, such as to provide guidance when developing components for use by many organizations.

Chapter 8, "Metrics for Reuse Libraries," looks at different metrics to consider when working with reuse libraries. Throughout the early history of software reuse, reuse library issues drove the research and technology in the field. This chapter explains the metrics that an organization will find useful when evaluating the success and use of a reuse library.

Finally, Chapter 9, "Measuring Reuse Across the Life Cycle," discusses measuring software in all phases of the software life cycle. As with reuse metrics for code, much of the difficulty with measuring reuse in other phases comes from trying to determine what counts as reuse and from gathering the necessary data.

Although metrics aim to objectively quantify the activities of an organization, applying metrics often leads to difficulties that extend far beyond the quantifiable. Every organization will face these difficult questions when putting together a metrics suite for its reuse program. This book addresses these issues in a straightforward, common-sense way that organizations can immediately put to use.

❖ ACKNOWLEDGEMENTS

I have had the privilege of working with many talented professionals at IBM, Loral Federal Systems, and Lockheed Martin Federal Systems. Many of the technical insights that I have described in this book have resulted from collaborating with my colleagues and friends. I must start by thanking Dr. Will Tracz for all the help he has given me, not only on this book but in so many of my other endeavors. I would also like to thank Marilyn Gaska for her strong leadership of the reuse program in Owego, Fred Illig for his tireless leadership of the reuse program in Springfield, Kathy Yglesias for so many important ideas over the years, Dr. Keith Werkman for collaborating with me on many reuse projects, and Allen Matheson for his excellent support of myself and our company's reuse program. Of course, I cannot understate the contributions of Dr. Joe Caruso, with whom I shared many of the challenges and successes expressed in this book.

Reuse rarely succeeds without management support. Fortunately, the Owego reuse program has always had managers and executives dedicated to reuse. I feel especially grateful for the professional and personnal support that I have received from Dr. Rodger Fritz and Dave Wales.

In many ways I have built on the hard work of others. To them I owe the experiences and much of the data that has gone into this book. This includes special thanks to Karen Parker, Reuse Coordinator of the Lockheed Martin CCTT program. However, I owe a debt to the entire former Reuse Technology Support Center (RTSC) and Corporate Reuse Council (CRC) of the IBM Corporation.

This book would not have happened without the excellent support of the publication team at Addison-Wesley. I would also like to thank the other reviewers for their valuable comments and suggestions. This book benefited from the insights of Kevin Benner, Allen Briggs, Dr. Scott Henninger, Andrew Rood, and Robin Rowe. I sincerely appreciate the work they put into their reviews.

Finally, I would like to thank my parents, family, and friends for encouraging me in everything I do.

Jeffrey S. Poulin
10 June 1996

❖ 1 ❖

Motivating Software Reuse Through Metrics

Many reports of industry reuse experiences show impressive benefits in terms of productivity, quality, costs, and cycle time. However, not one of these reports explains how these benefits were calculated. What the reports lack is a common model of what to count as reuse and how to assess the value of reuse. We will soon see how little faith we can put in metric values unless we understand how these reuse levels and benefits were quantified.

This book resulted from the need for such a model at IBM and, subsequently, many other organizations. Like many companies, we had a substantial investment in reuse based on good faith and the feeling that reuse "seemed like the right thing to do." However, no one could quantify how much reuse they did, much less whether or not they derived any benefit from it. Nearly every development site had a reuse program and staff, but no way to report or compare results. Consequently, the internal reuse community listed the lack of reuse metrics as *the number one problem* they faced. As expenses became harder and harder to justify, the problem became critical. This book contains answers for organizations that find themselves with a similar need to measure reuse levels and the benefits of their reuse metrics program.

❖ TERMS

It always helps to start by briefly explaining our use of terms. Even experienced reuse practitioners will benefit from reviewing this section, because many terms that we use very casually have traditionally had different meanings or connotations [79]. This section specifies how this book uses some of the major terms; see "Appendix C: Reuse Metric Glossary" on page 163 for a more comprehensive list. We will save the most difficult of all definitions, *how to define reuse*, for Chapter 4, "Defining Reuse from a Metrics Point of View," on page 33.

SOFTWARE COMPONENTS

We normally consider "software" reuse as the use of existing components of source code to develop a new software program, or *application*. In this sense, a group of people, or *organization*, reuses the existing components [51]. However, reusable software components can take many other forms, including executable programs, code segments, documentation, requirements, design and architectures, test data, test plans, and experience. With this in mind, we define a *reusable component* as a group of functionally related software modules and their associated documentation. For example, a *reusable component* may take the form of a software "building block" of routines and documentation that offers primitive operations on top of which programmers can develop more complex and specific capabilities [82].

BLACK-BOX VERSUS WHITE-BOX REUSE

Reuse takes two primary forms in an organization: either it happens by accident (opportunistic reuse) or the organization plans and designs reuse into their development process (systematic reuse).

Almost every organization practices opportunistic reuse by salvaging old information in some ad hoc fashion. People routinely save a little time by modifying existing software to make it fit their current need. However, this *white-box* reuse—copying and modifying software or components—has limited benefits. The modified component must undergo the same testing, configuration management, maintenance, documentation, and all the other requirements as a new component. In other words, white-box reuse achieves a marginal savings, which does not extend beyond the development phase.

On the other hand, an organization that practices systematic reuse plans and formally integrates reuse into a well-defined software development process. In systematic reuse, developers focus on the use of *black-box* assets, or unmodified software components. This means the developer does not alter the source files of the reusable component; if behavior modifications are necessary, the developer makes them all through parameter passing, generic instantiations, or (in the case of object-oriented languages such as C++), inheritance and polymorphism.

This book focuses on black-box reuse. As we will see in "Use of Modified Software" on page 46, the benefits of black-box reuse greatly exceed those of white-box reuse. The developer knows the component functions without error and can avoid significant effort, especially in the unit test through maintenance phases. Furthermore, the developer does not need to know the component's implementation. This raises the level of abstraction required to program, accelerates the learning curve, lowers the perceived software complexity,[1] and reduces the effort required to enhance and maintain the final product. A successful reuse program depends on having planned, systematic reuse of unmodified components as a key part of application development. Although we will periodically discuss white-box reuse, modifying existing software for use in new applications really falls into the category of *reengineering*.

REUSE CONSUMERS AND PRODUCERS

Reuse does not just involve the use of components from another application team or program. A successful reuse program requires someone to produce shareable components in the first place [10]. In short, a *reuse consumer* seeks to reduce costs through reusing the work products of others; a *reuse producer* works to increase the reusability of work products. Everyone working on a project must be a reuse consumer, identifying opportunities for reuse. When these are identified, it is usually most cost-effective to produce and maintain shared components by passing control of those components to a central team that performs these functions for the entire project. Chapter 6, "Implementing a Metrics Program," discusses how to organize development teams to support reuse and assign reuse responsibilities.

We want to have reuse metrics for both consuming and producing software. Most reuse metrics in use today only apply to reuse consumers because they measure the amount of reuse on a project. We also want to measure reuse producers; a complete set of metrics should provide indicators of the amount of useful reusable code produced on the project.

DOMAIN ANALYSIS AND ENGINEERING

Having a planned, systematic reuse process assumes the existence of software to reuse; domain analysis helps identify this software. A domain analysis primarily consists of a well-structured, intense study of a collection of related problems or a collection of related application programs. We call the area bounded by these problems or applications a *domain* [3]. A domain analysis helps answer the following questions:

1. What software can we reuse?
2. How do we make it reusable?

---

[1] We will occasionally use the term *complexity* to refer to the intuitive difficulty in understanding or working with a particular software component. We do not mean to suggest or endorse any general "complexity metric"; work in software measurement has invalidated much of the metrics in this area. However, we find the notion of a "complex" component useful just as we find the notion of a "reusable" component useful. See Chapter 7, "Measuring Software Reusability."

A domain analysis helps identify the common parts of a problem: those features which can later translate into reusable software. The domain analysis also helps develop an understanding of the problem; when documented, this understanding leads to models of the domain, preliminary design documents, and interface specifications.

The domain analysis process starts by characterizing and understanding the *problem space*. The analyst must factor out commonality in the problems so as to identify common threads. The analyst then attempts to characterize and understand the *solution space* for the domain. Finally, the analyst maps the problem space to the solution space by modeling a framework or reference architecture to generate applications within the domain [143]. *Domain engineering* extends domain analysis to include the actual construction of reusable software for the software system.

EXTERNAL AND INTERNAL REUSE

When we refer to internal and external reuse, we refer to *where* an organization or application obtained the software that it uses. When an organization or application program writes procedures or methods it developed for its own repeated use, we call it *internal reuse*. When an organization uses software it obtained from another source, such as another organization, we call it *external reuse*. We normally want reuse metrics to assess the level of reuse accomplished by a group of people, or how well that group performed reuse on an application. In this sense, an organization reuses software when it obtains the software from another organization or application. Software is reused by an application when an organization integrates a piece of software into the application that someone originally developed for use on another application.

However, not all people use these terms the same way. Because we call software within the static declaration scope of a program (of a structured programming language such as Pascal or Ada®)[2] "internal" to the program. Some reuse models refer to the use of a function or procedure within this scope as *internal reuse*. We will see in Chapter 4, "Defining Reuse from a Metrics Point of View," why we do not consider this fundamental practice in programming a form of reuse.

Many organizations may contribute to a large project. On such projects, we count the software that passes between organizations as reuse. Some references call this "internal reuse" of software because all the work falls internal to the project. This can lead to significant confusion when one person uses the word "internal" to mean "internal to a very large program" and another person uses the term to mean "using your own code." *This book will consistently use the latter interpretation*. In summary:

---

[2] Registered trademark of the U.S. Government Ada Joint Program Office.

- *External* reuse refers to the use of software obtained from another organization or software application. We normally only care about external reuse.
- *Internal* reuse refers to software developed and used repeatedly by the same people on the same application. We call this "good programming" and do not count it as reuse.

❖ EXPECTED LEVELS OF REUSE

Figure 1 shows the three classes of software that make up a typical software application. This model indicates the amount of reuse we expect in each class based on industry experiences in software development. The three classes represent the relative specificity of a component for solving a problem in software. The model shows that some software components are useful in a wide range of problem areas and applications; other software components have a more limited, though equally important, range of use. Starting with the most generic class:

1. **Domain-independent** software is the category with the widest useful range. Domain-independent software provides the foundation for programming: e.g., abstract data types (ADT), graphical user interface functions, and math libraries. Because this software spans many different application areas, or domains, we call the use of software from this class *horizontal reuse*. Reuse levels from horizontal reuse will not generally exceed more than about 20% of an application.

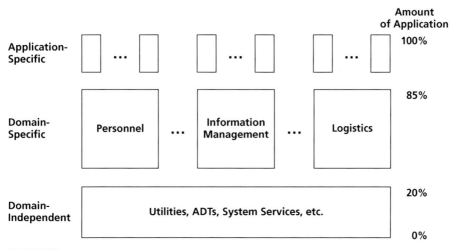

FIGURE 1 *The Three Classes of Software*

2. **Domain-specific** software contributes the most to reuse, but only *within the problem domain*. High-speed communications device drivers, navigational aids for aircraft, and financial services libraries serve as good examples of domain-specific software. Domain-specific software concentrates on an area of an organization's business processes; we call the use of software from this class *vertical reuse*. An organization must practice vertical reuse to move from a maximum reuse level of about 20% to the 85% level targeted by very successful reuse organizations.

3. Finally, **application-specific** software handles the unique details of a customer's requirements; it consists of the last 15% of a well-designed application. "Application-specific" generally means "custom code." Although opportunities exist to reuse software within an application team, this software tends to deal exclusively with how one application implements a function and typically has very limited reuse potential *even within its own domain*.

Understanding these classes can prove useful in several ways. First, they can help form a basis for developing an organizational reuse strategy. Second, the model can help the organization set realistic reuse goals and target the reuse of software based on where it finds itself in the development cycle; early in the cycle it might focus on building and reusing domain-independent software, whereas later in the cycle it might focus on domain analysis and engineering techniques. Finally, because the model creates a framework for expectations, a metrics analyst can assess reuse levels reported by the organization and in the literature and make an initial determination of their credibility.

❖ EXPECTED BENEFITS OF REUSE

Many sources expound on the expected benefits of reuse. As shown in Figure 2, the benefits span business and technical objectives and range from increased capacity to faster time-to-market. Published industry experiences seem to corroborate these expectations:

- **Nippon Electric Company** (NEC) achieved *6.7 times higher productivity* and *2.8 times better quality* through 17% reuse [67]. They *improved software quality 5–10 times* over a 7-year period through the use of unmodified reuse components in the domain of basic system software development and in the domain of communication switching systems [91].

- **GTE Corporation** *saved $14 million in costs* of software development with reuse levels of 14% [116].

- **Lower development costs**
- **Higher productivity**
- **Reduced cycle time**
- **Lower training costs**
- **Easier maintenance**
- **Higher quality**
- **Lower risk**
- **Better interoperability**

FIGURE 2 *Expected Benefits of Reuse*

- A study of 75 Ada projects in 15 firms totaling over 30M lines of code (LOC) found reuse resulted in *10 times higher quality* with reuse levels of 10–18% [124].

- **Toshiba** saw a *20–30% reduction in defects* per line of code with reuse levels of 60% [44].

- **DEC** *reported cycle times that were reduced by a factor of 3–5* through reuse levels of 50–80% [66].

- **Hewlett-Packard** (HP) cited quality improvements on two projects of *76% and 24% defect reduction, 50% and 40% increases in productivity,* and a *43% reduction in time-to-market* with *reuse levels up to 70%* [84].

- **CAP-Netron** documented over *90% reuse* from reusable MIS "frames" using COBOL [12].

- **Raytheon** achieved a *50% productivity increase* in the MIS domain from 60% reuse using COBOL [81].

- **Software Architecture and Engineering, Inc.** achieved *80–90% reuse* in distributed applications using C [43].

- A study of nine companies showed reuse led to *84% lower project costs, cycle time reduction of 70%,* and *reduced defects* [23].

To put these results into perspective, we must view the reported accomplishments within a common framework. This book will help us ask and understand questions such as "How did the organization measure the reuse?" "What did they count?" "If our organization did the same things, could we expect to see the same kinds of results?"

We believe that to achieve the results shown above, reuse must become fully integrated into the software development cycle. In short, we must *institutionalize reuse* so that it becomes "Business as Usual (BAU)" for the organization. A systematic reuse program can contribute to business success, and it is a fundamental premise of this book that reuse metrics play a key role in that program.

> **Reuse metrics can help achieve your reuse goals.**

❖ THIS BOOK WILL EXPLAIN . . .

This book will show the reader why metrics play such an important role in a reuse program. For example, in Chapter 4, "Defining Reuse from a Metrics Point of View," we put industry reuse reports into context, or more accurately, lack of context. We discuss what to measure as reuse and why. We use actual scenarios and anecdotes to explain the variances in measurement that appear in current journal articles and experience reports.

This book continues with an overview of major reuse metric and return-on-investment (ROI) models, along with their strengths and weaknesses. We then recommend a "starter set" of metrics for measuring reuse levels and the economic benefits of reuse. These simple and informative metrics require only easily observable and collectable data. Nonetheless, they work for a diverse collection of projects and companies worldwide.

This book continues with a discussion of metrics for software "reusability." Unlike reuse level and economic metrics, these metrics attempt to quantify the utility of a software component. However, despite much research, no one has identified a general-purpose reusability metric. This book surveys the approaches to help the reader identify software attributes that most researchers and practitioners agree lead to more "reusable" software. More importantly, we present a common model of reusability metrics which readers can use to evaluate and apply the various approaches.

This book then introduces metrics for use with reuse libraries. Like other reuse metrics, these must reflect the financial return produced by verifiable use of software retrieved from the library. We introduce a library return-on-investment metric that uses methods consistent with those discussed throughout this book.

Finally, this book addresses the issue of measuring reuse across the software life cycle. To do this, we need units of measure and a consistent counting method in each software development phase. We show how to use this information to derive a total level of life-cycle reuse.

One area that this book does not cover centers on reuse *process* metrics. Process metrics and models typically help managers evaluate the status of their organizations from a qualitative viewpoint; this book focuses on repeatable, verifiable measurement of reuse levels and benefits. For information on process models, i.e., reuse maturity and reuse capability models, see the work at the Software Productivity Consortium [33] and the Harris Corporation [78].

❖ 2 ❖

A Reuse Metrics Overview

In this chapter we first introduce some *goals* for a reuse metric program. Before deciding on a suite of metrics, we must have a clear definition of what the organization wants to achieve from the metrics. Does the organization want to have an *objective way to assess reuse levels*? Does it want to *motivate developers* to reuse software rather than develop it from scratch? Does it want to *estimate the benefits* of reuse as part of an investment plan for developing suites of related applications from reusable parts? Every organization will have unique goals, requirements, and priorities.

After discussing goals and requirements for reuse metrics, this chapter defines several major categories of reuse metric and economic models:

1. *Reuse Level Models*, which answer the question: "How much reuse did we do?"

2. *Reuse Leverage Models*, which answer the question: "How much better did we do with reuse?"

3. *Reuse Economic Models*, including:

   ♦ *Cost Avoidance Models*, which answer the question: "How much money did I not have to spend because I reused something rather than building it from scratch?"

   ♦ *ROI Models*, which analyze the net benefit of reuse after expending some level of resources. ROI models may show benefits in terms of any resource, such as effort (e.g., Labor-Months) or money; they often take into account the time value of money for longer-duration projects. ROI models answer the question: "What long-term economic justification does reuse offer?"

   ♦ *Cost–Benefit (C-B) Models*, which analyze reuse problems by itemizing all the cost factors influencing reuse, summing the values for these factors, and basing the business decision on the result. C-B models answer the question: "Should we do reuse at all?"

❖ METRIC GOALS AND REQUIREMENTS

We must first make it clear what we hope to accomplish through reuse measurement. When introducing a reuse program to an organization, we face an immediate problem when we walk into a development manager's office and start talking about expected benefits. Consider that over the past year or so managers have heard similar promises from a plethora of other groups: the Malcolm Baldrige team, the ISO-9000 team, the Total Quality Management (TQM) team, the Software Process Team, etc. Every one of these groups promises the same kinds of benefits that we do. However, the manager never sees any significant change. Part of the problem stems from the lack of measurements. Furthermore, no one can trace a specific action (e.g., reusing software) to a specific benefit (e.g., cost and schedule). The manager might say something like:

> "I've heard this all before. If I actually experienced all the cost savings and productivity improvements you promised, I wouldn't have a budget left nor people to work for me. Nothing ever comes of this stuff."

We can overcome this predisposition to doubt with a reasonable and easily understood presentation. We therefore propose the following list as major goals for reuse metrics. We place significant emphasis on *truthfulness* and *simplicity:*

1. **Provide *realistic* measures of reuse.** When we place a numeric value on our reuse accomplishments we want to have faith in that number. It should reflect our true reuse level without influence from other tangential factors.

2. **Estimate the benefits of reuse.** Nothing makes a believer out of people like seeing the benefits laid out in dollars. Metrics need to help us show the effect reuse has on the "bottom line." The metrics need to give reasonable, justified estimates.

3. **Provide feedback to developers and management.** Developers need a defined method to measure and to report on what they have done. People need feedback. This gives them a sense of accomplishment and helps define their mission. Feedback, however, must be prudent so as to maintain confidentiality where appropriate and not induce resentment.

4. **Give simple, easy-to-understand values.** Metrics should not require a specialist from accounting to interpret. Getting people to adopt a new technique or idea often depends on how well they comprehend it. People will more readily adopt metrics that they understand and that provide meaningful values.

5. **Have a minimal impact on business.** No one wants to make more work. Whatever data we need and metrics we generate must fit easily into the current business environment.

6. **Comply with the tenets of metric theory.**[3] The metrics should yield consistent, repeatable values independent of who calculates them and should prove mathematically and/or axiomatically sound [41, 146].

7. **Encourage reuse.** In general, metrics should serve, not a *prescriptive* role, but a *descriptive* one. They should objectively reflect attributes of the software, rather than telling people how to behave. However, metrics affect people's behavior, and because of this we have found metrics to play an important role in building a reuse program.

❖ REUSE PERCENT—THE DE FACTO STANDARD MEASURE OF REUSE LEVEL

Most people want to have a way to quantify the amount of reuse that took place on an application or within an organization. They want a way to measure *reuse levels.* Note that almost every experience report expresses reuse levels in terms of "reuse percent."[4] The equation for calculating percents uses only simple division, so reuse percent equals

$$\frac{Reused\ Software}{Total\ Software} \times 100\%$$

Although a *percent* does not tell us the amount of software reused, expressing reuse level as a percentage has a number of advantages. First, people find it easy to understand. As we read experience reports and hear discussions about the levels of reuse, we feel comfortable seeing reuse levels in terms of "percent." Second, as the equation above shows, anyone can easily calculate a reuse percent value with readily available information about a project.

Reporting reuse levels in terms of percent has become the de facto standard in industry. We see it and hear it all the time when people discuss software reuse. However, without any explanation of the data that makes up the metric, the metric has no meaning. Furthermore, without a consistent definition of the data and a repeatable method of obtaining it, a credible metric cannot exist. Experience reports cite pretty specific results based on software reuse. But:

---

[3] The details and importance of this statement probably do not interest the average practitioner. Among other things, the statement reminds us to ensure that our equations actually measure the attributes of software that we care about, and that the values they give do not do strange things—i.e., go down when we expect them to go up.

[4] An alternative, equivalent expression of reuse level expresses a reuse level of *n*% by its decimal equivalent. We call this expression of reuse level the *Reuse Ratio.*

No one defines what they count!

How do these companies measure their level of reuse? When we see these numbers in experience reports, how do we know where they came from? We will feel especially uncomfortable once we see in Chapter 4, "Defining Reuse from a Metrics Point of View," some of the ways organizations use metrics to misrepresent what they really do. Furthermore, without a standard definition of what counts and what does not, we cannot compare one report with another. Without this definition, we simply cannot believe many of the reports now in print.

❖ REUSE LEVERAGE MODELS

Although reuse level metrics play, perhaps, the most popular role in reuse metrics, they do not indicate the benefit resulting from the reported level of reuse. *Reuse Leverage* metrics take a step in the direction of expressing reuse benefits by showing the "multiplier" effect of reuse. Reuse Leverage works the same as *productivity indices*. In other words, it shows the benefit resulting from reuse relative to performing the same action without reuse.

Example: Assume an organization has no involvement in reuse whatsoever; we assign a value of 1 to the relative productivity of that group. If the group increases its productivity by reusing software, then the relative productivity of the organization will increase in proportion to the level of reuse. If the organization increases productivity by 20% due to reuse, we say it experienced a reuse leverage of 1.2.

$$Reuse\ Leverage\ = \frac{Productivity\ with\ Reuse}{Productivity\ without\ Reuse}$$

❖ REUSE ECONOMIC MODELS

Reuse economic models fall into one of three general categories. First, *cost avoidance models* seek to show the financial benefit of reuse in terms of money the reuser did not have to spend. In general, cost avoidance models apply to single teams or organizations. The second category, *return-on-investment (ROI) models*, shows reuse benefits in any terms, such as effort or costs, by giving the net cost or benefit of reuse. ROI models tend to apply to large projects as opposed to individual teams or organizations. The third category, *cost–benefit models*, attempts to itemize all the costs of reuse and balance them against the benefits.

COST AVOIDANCE

Because business decisions drive reuse and money drives business decisions, many reuse economic models seek to quantify reuse benefits in strictly financial terms. Most of these metrics use the term *cost avoidance* to distinguish reuse benefits from *cost savings*, because cost savings might imply that someone could afford to have their budget cut. (Most managers would rather take credit for "doing more with the same amount" than risk having to "do more with less.")

Cost avoidance emphasizes not expending resources. Unfortunately, organizations rarely have the ability to directly capture these costs. In part, this is because it is difficult to separate the contribution of reuse to an organization's performance from many other influencing factors. Reuse also results in numerous qualitative, hard-to-quantify benefits such as commonality of function, standardized user interface, and ease of maintenance. Finally, reuse can help meet aggressive cost and cycle-time targets. An organization cannot easily quantify the contribution of reuse to these targets.

Most cost avoidance models focus on individual teams or organizations. Cost avoidance models do not necessarily take into account the costs of reuse. They do this for several reasons: First, it is simpler. Second, the models tend to have a relatively limited scope, and so they can ignore costs that the parent organization might incur to support reuse. As reuse consumers, these organizations report only the benefit they receive. Cost avoidance models always return a result in financial terms.

ROI MODELS

Return-on-investment models differ from cost avoidance models in that they assume that the organization has committed or will soon commit resources to a reuse effort. The ROI analysis seeks to determine if that investment will pay off. In other words, will the organization realize a benefit that exceeds their investment?

ROI models tend to have a larger scope than cost avoidance models. They typically take into account the costs of building and maintaining company-wide reuse libraries, of providing an expert staff to consult on reuse issues, and of sponsoring groups to exclusively build reusable components. They consider the chances of amortizing costs across the entire organization based on the number of users and expected market for reusable software; etc. A ROI model also tends to take a long-term view of reuse, since an organization will normally use its tools and reusable software for many years. When an analysis spans 3–5 years or more, we need to consider the time value of money (interest rates, inflation, etc.).

ROI models account for these factors in a number of ways. One way involves determining the aggregate costs and benefits of reuse without necessarily itemizing each one as done in a cost–benefit analysis. The model then can apply a Net Present Value

(NPV) analysis to determine if the value of investment and compare the investment with other alternatives. Another method used by ROI models takes the general form [6, 123]:

$$ROI = \sum_{i=1}^{n} b_i \times (Reuse\ in\ Phase_i)$$

where *n is* the number of software life-cycle phases.

The coefficient b_i can reflect many different variables, such as the difficulty, complexity, or cost of doing reuse in *phase_i*. Unfortunately, we must determine the value of b_i by tuning the model for use in each organization. Proponents of these models usually provide suggested coefficient values to use when starting to tune the model.

COST–BENEFIT ANALYSIS

As the name implies, cost–benefit (C-B) analysis determines the value of reuse by first finding or estimating reuse costs and benefits. Once we have collected and tallied this information, we simply determine the total benefits and total costs by summing each benefit, B_i, and each cost, C_i:

$$Benefits = \sum_{i=1}^{n} B_i$$

$$Costs = \sum_{i=1}^{n} C_i$$

For completeness, we should gather this data for each possible software development approach (with and without reuse). We then consider all alternatives and recommend either of the following:

1. Invest in the most favorable alternative; or
2. Invest in reuse if the sum of benefits exceeds the sum of costs [10].

C-B analysis only looks at reuse activities, as opposed to examining the entire software effort. It requires assigning values to all known costs and benefits of reuse, including intangible items (e.g., quality), summing the values, and possibly applying a discount factor (Net Present Value analysis) depending on the time period of the analysis. The following tables show the kinds of information that a reuse analyst should consider collecting or estimating. As shown in Table 1, we can attribute many possible benefits to reusing software, and we can quantify many of those benefits in terms of finances or effort, such as Labor-Months (LMs). These benefits depend on the ability to reuse and amount of reuse during each software life-cycle phase. They include the benefits of reduced cycle time, such as the possibility of early product

TABLE 1 *Benefits of Reusing Software*

b_i	Description	Unit
b_1	Reduced cost to design	LMs × $/design
b_2	Reduced cost to document	pages × $/page
b_3	Reduced cost to implement	$/LOC
b_4	Reduced cost to unit test	LMs × $/LM
b_5	Reduced cost to design tests	LMs × $/LM
b_6	Reduced cost to document tests	pages × $/page
b_7	Reduced cost to implement tests	LMs × $/LM
b_8	Reduced cost to execute testing	LMs × $/LM
b_9	Reduced cost to produce publications	pages × $/page
b_{10}	Added revenue due to delivering product early	months × $/month
b_{11}	Reduced maintenance costs	errors × $/error
b_{12}	Added revenue due to improved customer sales	sales × $/sale
b_{13}	Reduced cost of tools	$
b_{14}	Reduced cost of equipment	$
b_{15}	Reduced cost to manage	LMs × $/LM

delivery and of increased sales. Other benefits include reduced need to purchase tools and equipment or to hire people to administer them.

Table 2, on page 16, itemizes many of the costs of reusing software. Not overlooking the impact of metrics, the list starts with the cost of performing an economic justification such as a C-B analysis. It includes the costs of domain analysis, an essential part of building a well-engineered suite of reusable parts. The costs include the costs of searching for, learning about, and integrating reusable software into a product and the costs of integration testing. Finally, some organizations simply purchase suites of reusable software; common examples include commercial collections of abstract data types [19], and graphical user interface components. The purchase costs, maintenance, and licensing fees of these products contribute to the costs of reuse.

Note that this list groups the costs of reusing software into categories that may, in turn, include many other unforeseen and very real costs. An enlightening experience report by a development team at Intermetrics helps emphasize the fact that "reuse does not come for free" [80]. They tell of the difficulty of reusing software while developing applications ranging from 20K to 200K LOC of Ada for use by the Navy in

TABLE 2 *Costs of Reusing Software*

c_i	Description	Unit
c_1	Cost of performing C-B analysis	LMs × $/LM
c_2	Cost of performing domain analysis	LMs × $/LM
c_3	Cost of locating and assessing reusable parts	LMs × $/LM
c_4	Cost of integrating reusable parts	LMs × $/LM
c_5	Cost of modifying reusable parts	LMs × $/LM
c_6	Cost of maintaining modified reusable parts	errors × $/error
c_7	Cost of testing modified reusable parts	LMs × $/LM
c_8	Fees for obtaining reusable parts	$
c_9	Fees or royalties for reusing parts	copies used × $/copy

Command, Control, Communications, and Intelligence (C3I) applications. In one case, the team located a reusable language translator component in a national reuse repository. After obtaining the component on diskettes, the team spent 10.25 person-hours on troubles with everything from not having the proper size diskette drive to missing a file which the translator required to run. In another case the team obtained a message-handling subsystem from another project and spent 12.5 hours porting it for demonstration at the customer environment. However, when fielding the component they found numerous fatal system dependencies built into the subsystem, such as dependence on certain operating system environmental variables and file security controls. They wasted hours on many other unexpected problems, such as source file incompatibility between the reuse and target software, and discovering that the reuse documentation only came in a format used by a proprietary word processor that no one in the office happened to use.

By providing standards and processes, a systematic reuse program can help control many of the problems faced by the Intermetrics team. However, as this experience shows, a reuser must often persist before seeing ultimate success. The stereotypical programmer might ask: "Why should I spend a couple of hours searching the reuse library to find an algorithm that would easily solve this problem when I can write it myself in a month or two?" We can use reuse metrics to show how investing that effort, or even much more, can have a very rewarding return.

In Table 3, we see some of the benefits of producing reusable software. Judging from this limited list, we can see why most organizations feel reluctant to produce reusable software as part of their normal development activities. Unless the organization plans to make a commercial product out of the reusable software and sell the product to a

TABLE 3 *Benefits of Producing Reusable Software*

b_i	Description	Unit
b_1	Added revenue due to income from selling	$\$ \times$ #users
b_2	Added revenue from fees or royalties	$\$ \times$ #users $\times$ #copies

significant market, they have little incentive. Most organizations will derive little or no benefit from producing reusable software for other organizations to use. High-level management and executives must recognize this situation and, if economic analysis justifies it, create a healthy reuse environment for the overall good of the company.

Table 4 demonstrates the problem of getting organizations to produce reusable software for use by other organizations in their company. This list shows the kinds of costs that the organization will incur. Furthermore, because reusers expect more complete documentation, higher quality, and well-abstracted components, these costs to design, model, implement, test, and document reusable components will exceed those to simply develop an equivalent component for use in one application. Note that this list of costs also includes those required to set up and maintain a reuse library in which to store the reusable components. The table ends with a very important item: the costs of marketing the software. Persistent and persuasive publicity makes developers aware of available reusable components and increases the likelihood that the developers will use the components at the next opportunity.

Unfortunately, we cannot consider even these extensive, comprehensive lists of costs and benefits as conclusive. For example, the lists exclude any training required to do things such as conduct domain analysis or use the reuse library. Furthermore, even though the lists suggest units to quantify each of the costs and benefits, much of the data simply will not exist. In these cases we need to estimate values for the terms or proceed with incomplete data. This situation severely dilutes any claims that our C-B analysis results in accurate or realistic conclusions.

Because of the amount of information required, conducting a thorough C-B analysis using a fully itemized accounting of each C-B term can require significant resources. Furthermore, because some of the information may not exist or may not be easily quantified, a full C-B analysis may not even yield a reliable result. For these reasons, we will next explore a way to abstract these costs and benefits into two useful values, the *Relative Cost of Reuse (RCR)* and the *Relative Cost of Writing for Reuse (RCWR)* [108].

TABLE 4 *Costs of Producing Reusable Software*

c_i	Description	Unit
c_1	Cost of performing cost–benefit analysis	LMs × $/LM
c_2	Cost of performing domain analysis	LMs × $/LM
c_3	Cost of designing reusable parts	LMs × $/LM
c_4	Cost of modeling/design tools for reusable parts	$
c_5	Cost of implementing reusable parts	$/LOC
c_6	Cost of testing reusable parts	LMs × $/LM
c_7	Cost of documenting reusable parts	pages × $/page
c_8	Cost of obtaining reuse library tools	$
c_9	Cost of added equipment for reuse library	$
c_{10}	Cost of resources to maintain reuse library	LMs × $/LM
c_{11}	Cost of management for development, test and library support groups	LMs × $/LM
c_{12}	Cost of producing publications	pages × $/page
c_{13}	Cost of maintaining reusable parts	LMs × $/LM
c_{14}	Cost of marketing reusable parts	$

❖ CONCLUSION

This chapter introduced reuse metrics and the economics of reuse. We have seen that although "Reuse Percent" has become the industry standard measure of reuse levels, very few reports tell what they counted as reuse. We need this information before we trust the values in the reports. Chapter 4 will address this issue.

This chapter then looked at the various approaches that reuse metrics take when assigning a value to the benefits of reuse. Reuse Leverage, a type of productivity index, shows how reuse "multiplies" the effectiveness of an organization. Reuse economic models take several forms: (1) cost avoidance, (2) return-on-investment, and (3) cost–benefit. Cost avoidance models put a value, in dollars, on reuse. ROI and C-B models help decide whether to invest in reuse by examining the finances of reuse and then comparing the result to a decision criterion. For example, after collecting all the costs and benefits of reuse, a C-B model tells us to invest in reuse if the total benefits exceed the costs.

Unfortunately, organizations may find it difficult or impossible to obtain all the information needed to use economic models. Some economic models contain multipliers and exponents designed to customize the output of the model to a particular situation. Organizations that use these models must calibrate the model with appropriate values for these multipliers and exponents.

The approach to reuse economics taken by C-B models requires the organization to know or estimate all the costs and benefits associated with reuse. This chapter provided example lists of the C-B factors related to consuming and producing reusable software. However, collecting this extensive data can prove expensive, and estimating what we cannot collect can adversely affect our confidence in the result. Chapter 3, "The Relative Costs of Developing with and for Reuse," will explain two useful abstractions that can help organizations avoid the need for this detailed information.

❖ 3 ❖

*The Relative Costs
of Developing
with and for Reuse*

Most people involved in software development will intuitively agree that reusing a software component will, in general, take less effort than writing an equivalent component from scratch. However, few people can quantify this difference. Does it take half as much effort? Does it take almost no effort at all? Does building a component explicitly for reuse by others take the same amount of effort as building it for one-time use? If not, how much more does it cost?

One way to determine this difference in effort involves actually completing the same project in two ways: once with reuse and once without. Very few organizations have the resources or motivation to do this. Instead, we may compare the results of a software development experience with reuse to a similar experience without reuse. By comparing statistics on development costs and schedules from these projects, we can see how much less time it takes to write software *with* reusable components and how much more time it takes to build software *for* reuse by others. We call these two abstractions the *Relative Cost of Reuse (RCR)* and the *Relative Cost of Writing for Reuse (RCWR)*.

To estimate the effects of reuse, we could conduct an extensive cost–benefit analysis as discussed in the previous chapter. Alternately, we could use RCR and RCWR to reach approximately the same conclusions. This chapter explains the concepts of RCR and RCWR and gives extensive experience reports on values for the two terms. Subsequent chapters will show how to use RCR and RCWR in reuse economic models.

❖ THE RELATIVE COST OF REUSE

Reuse does not come for free. In order to reuse software, the reuser must (1) locate, (2) understand, (3) integrate, (4) system test, (5) etc., with the reused component. As we will see, this typically takes about 20% of the effort required to write the same component from scratch. In this case the relative cost to reuse the component equals 0.2, and we have saved 80% of the development effort.

> **Definition:** Assume the cost to develop a new component equals one unit of effort. We call the portion of this effort that it takes to reuse a similar component *without modification* (black-box reuse) the *Relative Cost of Reuse (RCR)*.

EXPERIENCE REPORTS: RELATIVE COST OF REUSE

We can obtain fairly reliable values for RCR by observing the amount of effort required to integrate a reusable component into a system and then comparing that effort to that we would have needed in order to develop the component. For example, if it historically takes an organization 1000 hours to produce a 2000-line component that the same organization successfully integrated in only 200 hours, we would calculate an RCR of 0.2. This does not take into account variations in the relative complexity of the integrated components (or other environmental factors), but allows the organization to establish approximate values for RCR.

By collecting enough RCR values we can observe trends, identify the factors that affect RCR, and determine a median value upon which we can base a more statistically significant meaning. For example, Tracz states the costs of learning to reuse software as being 20–25% of the costs to write it new [140]. Margano reports RCR = 0.2 on the Federal Aviation Administration's Advanced Automation System (AAS) [88, 89]. Gaffney and Durek estimate that it costs 3–20% of a code object's construction cost to incorporate it into an application without modification [47]. Grady reports reuse takes 25% of the effort of writing new code at Hewlett-Packard (HP) [54]. Also reporting on the reuse program at HP, Lim reports reuse costs 19% of new development [84]. In this case, Lim cites results from two projects within HP. The first project involved a 55K LOC program for large-application software resource planning completed in Pascal and SPL. The second involved a 20K LOC enhancement and maintenance project for plotters and printers completed in C.

The European Consultants Network used Ada to implement dialogue management tools for workstations. In an excellent study, Favaro presents one of the best discussions on the relative costs of reuse [39]. The study had the primary goal of experimentally determining the values of RCR and RCWR (in the European Consultants Network terminology, the *component integration cost* and the *development cost as a reusable component*). As part of the analysis Favaro recognized the difficulty of accounting for how component "complexity" affects reuse. In other words, the values for RCR and RCWR would vary depending on the "complexity" of the component.

For the purpose of this study, Favaro classified reusable components into groups based on the following taxonomy of complexity:

1. *Monolithic* components (e.g., stacks, queues) have relatively simple and easy-to-manage structures.

2. *Polylithic* components (e.g., trees, lists) have more complex, recursive structures.

3. *Graph* components contain the most complex structures and require several types of traversal strategies.

4. *Menus* and *masks* represent the end products of the project and therefore include the most complex software to develop and to reuse. A menu accepts data input from the user, and a mask manages forms for data output.

As shown in Table 5, the study concluded that the cost of reuse ranged from 10 to 40% of new software costs, depending on the complexity (as defined in the list) of the reused software.

The results show that monolithic components, which have simple structures, require very little effort (RCR = 0.1) to understand and to integrate into a program. The slightly more complex polylithic components, which use aliases and private typing (in their Ada implementations) to make the components more generic, require a correspondingly greater amount of effort and have an RCR of 0.15. Graphs require even more time to understand and integrate, resulting in an even higher RCR of 0.25. The complex menus and masks required the greatest integration efforts, RCR = 0.3 and RCR = 0.4, respectively.

In an electronic switching system for telecommunications at AT&T Bell Labs, Ramesh and Rao show justification for an RCR of 20%, the factors that affect RCR, and a table showing how RCR can vary based on environmental factors [120]. In their case study, they combined reusable components as an aid to rapid prototyping. Like Favaro, they found that four basic assumptions hold when using a single RCR value of 0.2:

TABLE 5 *European Consultants Network—RCR*

Type of Software	*RCR*
Monolithic	0.10
Polylithic	0.15
Graph	0.25
Menu	0.30
Mask	0.40

1. The programmer understands both the source and target systems.
2. The reusable component does not contain very complicated abstractions.
3. The reusable components consist of relatively small amounts of code.
4. The reusable component came with good documentation.

In a comprehensive statistical study of a NASA software production environment doing ground support software for unmanned spacecraft in FORTRAN, Selby reports on numerous factors influencing the reuse of software components [131]. As part of this study, Selby collected data on 25 moderate and large software systems. These systems ranged in size from 3000 to 112,000 lines of FORTRAN. Of the 7188 modules in the study, NASA reused 17.1% without modification, 10.3% with less than (approximately) 25% modification, and 4.6% with major modification (more than about 25%). For developing software with reusable components, Selby found that the average module required 21.35 hours to develop from scratch, whereas to reuse a module without modification only required 0.58 hours. This leads to an RCR of .03.

In an excellent example of domain-specific reuse and product-line development, Bardo *et al.* at Loral Federal Systems report on an extensive reuse effort with software for constructing avionics simulators and trainers. Working in Ada and in C, the engineers built a generic software requirements specification, software architecture, and set of configurable reusable components. The project budgeted 5% of new development costs to allow for reconfiguring and integrating the reusable components into a new system. The engineers found this cost sufficient as they worked on each successive program and became familiar with the components [9].

SUMMARY: RELATIVE COST OF REUSE

The previous reports present RCR values for the reuse of unmodified components. Although the definition of reuse does not include the reuse of modified components, we may find it interesting to see the relative costs of incorporating components *with* modification. Selby found that whereas it took (on average) only 0.58 hours to incorporate a reusable component without modification, it took 8.62 hours to do the same with modification, even if the developer changed less than 25% of the component. This *RCR with Modifications* = .4 represents a *factor of 15 penalty* for making even slight modifications to a reusable component. Furthermore, if the amount of modification exceeded 25%, *RCR with Modifications* = .9 and the amount of effort to develop increased to 19.36 hours: a *penalty of 33 times the effort of black-box reuse!* In addition, Selby found that the average effort to make significant modifications to a component was only slightly less than that required to simply build the component from scratch (which took an average of 21.35 hours).

TABLE 6 *Summary of Relative Cost of Reuse (RCR) Values*

Organization	RCR
Favaro	0.1–0.4
Gaffney and Durek	0.03–0.2
Grady	0.25
Lim	0.19
Margano	0.20
Ramesh and Rao	0.20
Selby	0.03
Tracz	0.2–0.25
Bardo *et al.*	0.05

NOTE: Rajlich and Silva give an RCR for reuse with modifications of 0.4. Selby also reports RCR with slight modifications of 0.4.

In a report on domain-specific reuse in the domain of visual interactive tools using C and C++, Rajlich and Silva cite the relative cost of reuse for modifying old code at 0.4 [118, 119]. This relative effort represents a 60% savings over new development, clearly much less of an advantage than is achievable via unmodified reuse. Coupled with Selby's results, these findings clearly question the advantage of modifying a candidate reusable component over that of using it without change.

Table 6 summarizes the results of these RCR reports. In several instances the reports cite a range of values, which emphasizes the fact although the RCR provides us with a very useful abstraction, its actual value depends on numerous factors and environmental conditions. Looking at the values in table, we see that the median value in the reports falls at about 0.2. From this we conclude that:

> **Reusing software takes 20% of the effort of new development, so:**
> **RCR = 0.2.**

❖ THE RELATIVE COST OF WRITING FOR REUSE

Writing reusable components requires additional effort beyond simply writing a component for one-time use. As shown in Table 4 on page 18, the reuse producer must do the following:

1. Conduct a domain analysis,

2. Generalize for additional requirements,

3. Add more detailed documentation,

4. Test to increase trust,

5. Test for additional potential uses, and

6. Prepare the component for distribution.

Like the RCR, the RCWR abstracts these activities into a single term. As an example of how to use the RCWR, assume that it requires approximately 50% additional effort to develop a reusable component over the effort required to write the same component for one-time use. In this case the relative cost of writing for reuse equals 1.5.

> **Definition:** Assume the cost to develop a new component for one-time use equals one unit of effort. We call the portion of this effort that it takes to write a similar "reusable" component the *Relative Cost of Writing for Reuse (RCWR).*

Unfortunately, obtaining accurate and reliable values for the RCWR takes considerable effort. The following experience reports reflect observations made by groups that have developed software for reuse. We will use these experience reports to arrive at a general value for the RCWR.

EXPERIENCE REPORTS: RELATIVE COST OF WRITING FOR REUSE

Based on extensive reuse experiences on projects throughout IBM, Tracz gives a breakdown of the cost of making software reusable as follows [140]:

> 25% for additional generalization
> 15% for additional documentation
> 15% for additional testing
>   5% for library support and maintenance
> _____
> 60% additional cost to make software reusable

This results in RCWR = 1.6. We see that Tracz observes that "additional generalization" leads to the greatest cost increase of any of the reuse-related activities. This makes sense because the additional generalization introduced during design will determine the usefulness of the component on subsequent projects.

The Computer Sciences Corporation (CSC) reports that writing for reuse on the Federal Aviation Administration's Advanced Automation System (AAS) costs twice as much as creating one-time-use software [89]. Reporting actual data on a very large development project, Margano and Lindsey sought to dispel the common reason

TABLE 7 *Computer Sciences Corporation—RCWR*

Phase of development cycle	Percent of total cycle	Additional effort
High-level design	13%	10–15%
Low-level design	37%	60%
Code	20%	12.5%
Test	30%	12.5%
Totals	100%	100%

NOTE:
(1) Additional design effort depends on code complexity.
(2) 25% additional effort split between Code and Unit Test.
(3) **RCWR = 2.**

given by management for not encouraging the development of reusable components. Although the success of their program in many ways depended on software reuse, the up-front costs caused major concern. However, they realized that this strict short-term view overemphasized the cost of reuse relative to its benefit.

As seen in Table 7, Margano went into considerable detail analyzing the costs of developing for reuse by breaking down the additional effort by phase of the software life cycle. For example, the high-level design phase took 13% of the software life cycle and incurred an additional 10–15% level of effort when a component was built for reuse. Corroborating Tracz's observation, Margano also shows low-level design as the major cost driver in building components for reuse, with as much as 60% additional effort. Taken in their entirety, developing software for reuse resulted in an RCWR of 2.0.

In the same study described earlier in the RCR section, the European Consultants Network studied the relative costs to develop reusable software for workstation dialogue management tools [39]. As shown in Table 8, Favaro classified components by their complexity and showed RCWR cost factors ranging from 1.0 to 2.2.

The results show that monolithic components have such simple structures that they require essentially no extra effort to develop as reusable components (RCWR = 1.0). However, the RCWR values increase with the complexity of the components because of difficulties with engineering for reuse and with debugging time. Polylithic components show only slightly more effort to develop for reuse (RCWR = 1.2); however, the complex menu and mask take *about twice as much effort* to develop for reuse as they do to develop for simple one-time use.

In an extensive reusable software effort dating back to 1981, IBM dedicated a team of developers in Böblingen, Germany, to researching reusable design and implementing reusable components for use across the corporation [13]. The effort resulted in seven

TABLE 8 *European Consultants Network—RCWR*

Type of software	RCWR
Monolithic	1.0
Polylithic	1.2
Graph	1.6
Menu	1.9
Mask	2.2

abstract data type "Building Blocks" in the BB/LX language; the team has since implemented a suite of abstract data types in C++. The original building blocks contain about 10 different implementation features and combine the use of generic characteristics with the ability to derive abstract data types from similar existing ones. Each building block comes with a complete set of documentation, including specifications, test cases, and integration instructions. Furthermore, the development team in Böblingen fully supports the components in case of errors or questions. Most importantly, in more than 10 years of extensive use of the approximately 80K LOC of BB/LX reusable software, *no errors have ever appeared* [36]. Using cost and schedule data collected over this time, the Böblingen team reports that it costs up to twice their standard development costs to build reusable software of this quality, with the ratio of effort ranging from 1.25 to 2.0 and having a median of 1.5 [82]. This data supports IBM's RCWR value of 1.5.

In the same report that showed an RCR of 0.19 at Hewlett-Packard, Lim reports that developing for reuse costs 111–180% extra at HP [84]. Lim used data from projects developing firmware for use on instrument and graphics applications. Both of these domains represent significant areas of reuse potential within core HP product lines.

Reifer conducted an extensive analysis of data on the Ada programs to study the effects of using Ada in large program development. For this study Reifer obtained and used data from 30 completed Ada projects in 5 large U.S. aerospace firms. He later updated this data with experiences from an additional 45 projects completed by 10 firms and with data from 75 projects representing over 30 million lines of Ada code. As part of his findings, Reifer reported that it costs on average cost of 10–20% more to build a component for reuse [124].

In their work on avionics simulators and trainers, Bardo *et al.* also report that it took 15–25% additional effort to develop reusable versus application-specific components [9], an RCWR of 1.15–1.25. However, the Lockheed Martin Federal Systems developers did not gather explicit metrics; they based these costs on estimates.

Also working in Ada, Lockheed Martin Federal Systems (LMFS) has developed extensive suites of reusable software for use in various domains. On one large, complex project in the domain of Management Information Systems (MIS), LMFS designed and built a common services layer of reusable software prior to developing the applications that would use the software. Using three years of quantitative data from this project, LMFS calculated an RCWR of 1.86 [112].

Pant *et al.*, conducted a pilot experiment to assess the additional effort required for the generalization of object-oriented (OO) components [100]. They tested a number of statistical research hypotheses related to the correlation between different traditional metrics for OO programs, software development, and generalization effort and the change in size of classes as a result of generalization. They concluded that two opposing forces affect size upon generalization: completion of abstractions, which tends to increase size, and developing inheritance structures, which generally decreases class size. The results indicate that on average, generalization costs 55% more than original development, resulting in an RCWR of 1.55.

SUMMARY: RELATIVE COST OF WRITING FOR REUSE

As with values for RCR, experience reports may give values for RCWR but not necessarily substantiate the values with experimental or quantitative evidence. For example, reporting on the reuse state-of-the-practice, Caldwell gives some anecdotal evidence of reuse experiences showing additional costs of writing for reuse of 25–30% in the U.S. Department of Defense [23]. Gaffney and Cruickshank assume an additional cost factor of 1.5 for aerospace applications written in Ada [48]. Capers Jones reports that approximately 50% additional effort and a 30% longer schedule are required to write reusable components [70].

Table 9 summarizes the results of these RCWR reports. The values have a wide range from 1.0 to 2.2, indicating that effort required to write software depends on many factors such as how well the developers understand the domain in which they work. Nonetheless, RCWR provides a useful abstraction for generalizing the costs of developing software for reuse. Looking at the values for RCWR, we see that the median RCWR value for these reports falls at about 1.5. From this we conclude that:

> *Writing software for reuse takes 50% extra effort, so:*
>   **RCWR = 1.5.**

TABLE 9 *Summary of Relative Cost of Writing for Reuse (RCWR) Values*

Organization	RCWR
Caldwell	1.25–1.3
Favaro	1.0–2.2
Gaffney and Cruickshank	1.5
IBM	1.25–2.0
Jones	1.5
Lim	1.11–1.8
Margano	2.0
Reifer	1.1–1.36
Tracz	1.6
Bardo *et al.*	1.15–1.25
Lockheed Martin	1.86
Pant *et al.*	1.55

❖ CALCULATING YOUR OWN VALUES FOR RCR AND RCWR

Most organizations will probably find it easiest to base values of RCR and RCWR on the industry experiences above. However, if your organization has enough historical data, you may find the most accurate values for the RCR and RCWR by deriving them from your own organizational experience. Organizations with detailed budget data may already have the information they need in their contract management department or cost accounting system. For RCWR, we simply look up the cost of developing reusable code and compare it to the cost of developing all other code. We must use the same method to obtain both values: for example, the development team costs divided by the number of lines they wrote. We then find the RCWR by:

$$RCWR = \frac{Cost\ of\ code\ written\ for\ reuse\ by\ others}{New\ code\ cost}$$

Organizations that do not have separate cost data for the development of reusable software will have to take a slightly more complicated approach. First, we isolate the total software development costs on a project from other project costs. Assuming that the total amount of software on the project comes from:

New software + *Reused software* + *Code written for reuse by others*

We want to find the *Total Project Cost* such that:

$Total\ Project\ Cost\ =$

$New\ code\ cost\ \times\ New\ software\ +$

$RCR\ \times\ New\ code\ cost\ \times\ Reused\ software\ +$

$RCWR\ \times\ New\ code\ cost\ \times\ Code\ written\ for\ reuse\ by\ others$

With adequate historical data we can now solve for the RCR and RCWR. Alternatively, by using data from the following:

1. A project that reused software but did not produce any software for reuse, or

2. A project that built software for reuse but did not reuse any software,

we can reduce the number of unknowns in the equation to one and solve for the unknown value. For example, consider a project which reused software but did not build any software for reuse [32]. Then:

$Total\ Project\ Cost\ =$

$New\ code\ cost\ \times\ New\ software\ +\ RCR\ \times\ New\ code\ cost\ \times\ Reused\ software$

We can solve for RCR because we know the *Total Project Cost* and *New code cost* data for the project. By obtaining data from multiple projects and averaging the RCR values, we can increase our (statistical) confidence in the result.

❖ CONCLUSION

This chapter introduced two useful abstractions for addressing the costs and benefits of reuse. We call these two abstractions the *Relative Cost of Reuse (RCR)* and the *Relative Cost of Writing for Reuse (RCWR)*. The RCR represents the cost of reusing software as compared to writing the same software again; an RCR of 0.2 means it only takes 20% of the effort to reuse than it takes for new development. RCWR represents the additional cost we incur when building software for others to use. If it takes 50% more effort to generalize the design, write integration instructions, etc., then we say that RCWR = 1.5.

This chapter cited extensive experience reports that gave ranges of values for RCR and RCWR. By looking at these reports we found that RCR = 0.2 and RCWR = 1.5 make good, general default values for these two metrics. Organizations can use these default values when estimating the benefits of their reuse programs. This chapter also gave a method that an organization can use to calculate its own values for RCR and RCWR, if necessary. We will use the default values in examples throughout the book.

❖ 4 ❖

Defining Reuse from a Metrics Point of View

Any metric for reuse level must define what to measure and what *not* to measure. Without that definition, the metric has no meaning. This chapter discusses many different types and sources of the software that make up an application or product. In effect, it builds a spectrum of reuse from what we clearly should not count to what we clearly should. At one end of this spectrum lies software we should clearly not include in our reuse metrics, such as the operating system or language compilers. At the other end of the spectrum lies software that we clearly should count, such as software we obtain from reuse repositories or have constructed after extensive domain analysis and engineering. The real difficulty in "Defining Reuse from a Metrics Point of View" comes when deciding where to draw the line on this spectrum [105].

Deciding what to count and what not to count may sound easy, but in reality, it is a difficult and emotional issue. As soon as senior managers and executives make it known that they support reuse and then ask to see metrics that show how each of their organizations actually perform with respect to reuse, "what to count" becomes very important. Every organization realizes that if it wants to "look good" it will have to report a high reuse level. Managers will make it known that "if it looks like, smells like, or sounds like reuse . . . count it as reuse!" A clear definition of what to count as a "Reused Source Instruction" (RSI) helps guarantee uniformity of results and equity across organizations.

The counting model that follows does not represent the only answer, or necessarily the best answer, for any particular organization. However, the model reflects the questions faced when establishing a reuse metrics program and ultimately outlines the decisions that every organization must make. As a point of reference, representatives from nearly *every single development site in IBM* unanimously agreed to the definitions that follow. Furthermore, the Department of Defense Information Systems Agency (DISA) subsequently adopted these definitions with only minor modifications. The acceptance of this model did not come easily and in some respects will only come within an organization following a painful, in-depth exploration of the issues by all the personnel involved.

Note that this book uses *lines of code (LOC)* as the unit of measure. As a unit of measure, LOC values have known deficiencies, but they also serve as reliable indicator of overall software effort. Because we can automate their measurement, we can simplify data collection and improve consistency. Finally, most companies have a history of reporting software metrics such as productivity and quality in terms of LOC. Organizations such as the Software Productivity Consortium recommend using LOC for managing software projects [32]. Rather than attempt to change this culture, this book will work within the existing metric framework.

This does not mean that the paradigm depends on LOC as a unit of measure. If a company reports in terms of objects, function points, person-months, or whatever, the same ideas hold. The counting framework presented in the sections that follow simply outlines a method and rationale for defining reuse from a metrics point of view. See the discussion of question 4, "What if we don't use LOC?" on page 55 for details and issues related to using units other than LOC.

❖ THE BOUNDARY PROBLEM

Reuse occurs when someone avoids having to write software by obtaining and using software from someplace else. We call this *external reuse*. External reuse has two flavors. The first flavor reflects an organizational view of reuse; e.g., one organization uses software from another organization. The second flavor reflects a product view of reuse; e.g., Product A contains software the developers of Product A obtained from Product B.

The same organization that now develops Product A may have developed Product B. Nonetheless, we still classify this use of software as external reuse because the product uses software originally developed for use "someplace else." Most metric reports reported in the literature reflect *product* metrics. Although this book will differentiate the two when it matters, the two flavors overlap considerably.

The situation becomes more complex when we introduce *internal reuse*, or the repeated use of software within the same organization or product. For small organizations, professionals call this practice "good programming." In large organizations, what we call *internal reuse* becomes confusing because of the difficulty of managing large software development efforts that may span many suborganizations. These suborganizations may share software that we consider *internal* to the project.

In short, the essence of the external versus internal reuse question reveals itself when we try to decide when software comes from "someplace else." This book calls this question the *boundary problem*. After we see how to solve the boundary problem using organization/software boundaries, we will see the consequences of ignoring boundaries altogether.

ORGANIZATION/SOFTWARE BOUNDARIES

Our solution to the boundary problem comes from observing software development in a large organization. We see that unplanned reuse routinely happens when people interact frequently; e.g., office mates and team members swap and share code. As the frequency and quality of communication decreases, so does this kind of opportunistic reuse [18].

To distinguish the level at which software exchanges normally take place and at what level they do not, we observed that informal reuse (software sharing) commonly happens *within* organizations, such as departments and programming teams. However, sharing software *between* organizations happens much less often. Organizations experience many natural inhibitors to exchanging information, such as geography (different sites or buildings) and reporting structure (different managers). We want to encourage and measure reuse across these organizations.

This approach to the boundary problem has an added appeal because organizational structures almost always have a one-to-one correspondence to the structure of the software developed. In other words, *Organization A* has responsibility for developing *Application A*, or *Development Team B* has responsibility for *Software System B*. For example, at the Rockville division of Lockheed Martin Federal Systems, teams of 15–20 programmers have responsibility for developing specific software subsystems. These subsystems make up the aviation software developed at the site for the Federal Aviation Administration (FAA). Because we do not normally expect these teams to work together and share components, these teams have a "boundary" between them. Therefore, when one team uses another team's software, we count it as (external) reuse. When a team develops software for its own (internal) use, we do not count it as reuse.

With boundaries, reuse levels depend on organizational structure, because organizational structure determines when reuse takes place. In practice we almost always find an obvious and appropriate choice of boundary. This means that the resulting reuse metrics will reflect what the organization considers as reuse.

IGNORING THE BOUNDARY PROBLEM

What happens if we ignore the boundary problem? If we do, the reuse levels obtained can vary greatly. To see how this can happen we will examine the situation at the extremes: first, in a very large development effort, and second, in a very small effort.

Assume a 1 million line system consisting of 50 equal-size subsystems of 20K LOC with each subsystem assigned to a team of 8–12 programmers. Ignoring boundaries on a large system such as this could result in a number of interpretations of reuse. First, if we only count reuse from external sources we will probably obtain a very low reuse level. In this interpretation, ignoring boundaries gives us a result equivalent to setting a boundary at the system level. On the other hand, if we decide to count sharing of software across teams as reuse, we will obtain a higher reuse level. This interpretation sets reuse boundaries at the programming team level. If we ignore boundaries, then the resulting reuse report could end up using any combination of these two interpretations.

Now assume a team of three programmers working on a 5K LOC program. They obtain some software from the Internet and also write some functions that they repeatedly use. Ignoring boundaries again leaves the reuse level open to interpretation; the programmers could report the use of their own functions as reuse. On the other hand, if we use organizational boundaries, then all reuse comes from outside the team. Since we only have one organization, all reuse comes from the Internet software.

Note that the preceding discussion of organizational and counting boundaries uses arguments similar to those presented by the Function Point community [65]. As with Function Points, the boundary establishes the scope of the metric. If an organization has already established a metric program based on Function Points, then the organization will probably want to use the same application boundary for reuse metrics that it does for Function Point counting.

THE BOUNDARY PROBLEM: SMALL PROJECTS VERSUS LARGE PROJECTS

Figure 3 shows how reuse occurs on small projects. On a small project, all reuse comes from sources external to the Development Team. If the Development Team "would have written" a component, but did not have to because they acquired a reusable component from someplace else, then they experienced a benefit of reuse. For example, when the Development Team retrieves and uses two different software components from the company reuse library, then each component counts as reuse. When the Development Team acquires and uses software from other projects, it also counts the use of that software as reuse. In short, software crossing the Development Team boundary counts as reuse.

Now consider how organizations reuse software on large projects. As on small projects, teams working on a large project continue to find components for reuse in the company reuse library and from other projects. However, the teams can also obtain components for reuse from other teams working on the same project. Ideally

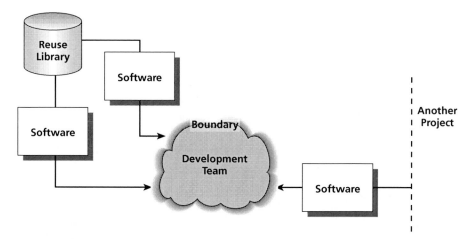

FIGURE 3 *Internal and External Reuse on a Small Project*

all teams share information, but in practice they cannot because of inefficient communication, geographic distribution, management structure, etc. Figure 4 illustrates how this works. Team A reuses software that it obtained from the reuse library, from another project, and from Team D on the same project. Team B also reuses two components from the reuse library; Team A happens to have used one of these components. Team C reuses the same software that Team A used from the other project as well as software developed by Team D. Team D does not reuse any software; in this figure Team D acts as a supplier of reusable components. Note that software that crosses the team boundaries counts as reuse. Software developed by a team and used within the team does not count.

To emphasize, this boundary (which a component must cross to be reused) depends on the situation, but almost always becomes obvious when we look at the organization (whether we call them programming teams, application teams, departments, Functional Groups, Operational Units, or whatever).

Example: A multinational software development company mobilizes its worldwide resources to develop a large distributed network management system. Following an extensive requirements definition phase, customer reviews, architecture development, and validation, dozens of software development departments have embarked on the design and implementation of their portions of the project. The departments communicate using state-of-the-art technology, but because of their geographical distribution, time zone differences, management structure, language differences, and missions, these teams will not, in general, share software.

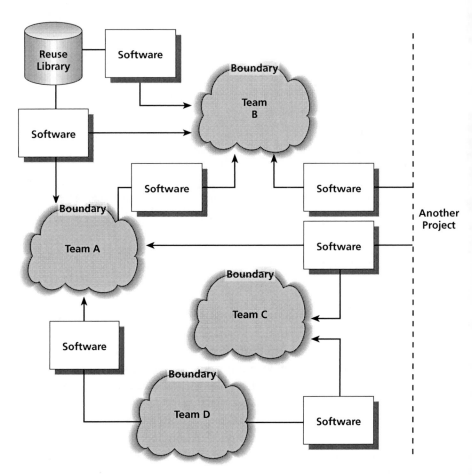

FIGURE 4   *Internal and External Reuse on a Large Project*

Therefore, we have determined that these departments form the appropriate reuse boundary for calculating reuse metrics on the project.

During the project, Department 23 from the company Database Division in Cary, NC, writes a component C for reuse that Department 39 from the Network Division in La Gaude, France, uses. We add component C to the list of components reused by Department 39. At the same time, Department 87 from the GUI development team in Rome, Italy, also reuses C. We add component C to the list of components reused by Department 87.

In summary, on small projects one organization develops the entire software product, and we can clearly define "external" and "internal" reuse. However, on large projects many organizations may contribute to the software project. So, software "external" to these organizations may happen to fall "internal" to the project. We want to measure reuse when the use of software saves effort. Remember that:

> **Organizational structure determines when reuse takes place!**

❖ WHAT TO MEASURE AS REUSE

We now will look at various categories of software, discuss why or why not each might count as reuse, and then give a recommended solution. Most of the conclusions hinge on whether or not we expect someone to write that software.

As we discuss these issues and reach our conclusions, we will define what it means when we refer to a Reused Source Instruction (RSI). Some of the choices may seem clear, but none have gone without controversy. For each code category, *someone has published a report claiming the category represents reuse!*

PRODUCT MAINTENANCE: NEW VERSIONS

Some argue that maintenance should count as reuse. Should Version 1.2.3 of Product X "reuse" Version 1.2.2 of the product? Imagine a 98K LOC product that adds 2K LOC of fixes and enhancements to its next version. Does it report 98% reuse? Most software metrics for product releases exclude data pertaining to the product *base.*[5] In this case, software metrics should reflect the effort on the 2K LOC of new and changed code. Likewise, reuse metrics should reflect the amount of the 2K LOC obtained from "someplace else" and should not claim the 98K LOC as reuse.

> **We do not count product maintenance as reuse.**

USE OF OPERATING SYSTEM SERVICES

Does use of operating system (OS) services constitute reuse? For example, if we store program data in files, does this mean we "reuse" the operating system or the file system? We clearly do not expect programmers to develop a new operating system for every program.

---

[5] The product base consists of all code previously released in the product.

> **We do not count use of the operating system as reuse.**

Over time, commonly used functions have migrated into the operating system as basic services. Before these services appeared in the OS they may have counted as reuse. In the future, their use will not count as reuse because the OS provides the service. Of course, not all operating systems support the same services, just as not all programming languages provide the same programming features. This point serves to illustrate how our approaches to programming and our views of reuse evolve.

USE OF HIGH-LEVEL LANGUAGES

The use of high-level languages (HLLs) raises two issues, the first somewhat simpler than the second. First, do we receive some "reuse" from the use of HLLs? HLLs have contributed to about a fivefold increase in programmer productivity [21]. Should a program written in C++ claim reuse of the compiler software, or, should we claim the output of a compiler as reuse because a compiler generates machine code from an HLL [5]? We do not claim reuse of HLL compilers for the same reasons we do not count use of the operating system: we do not expect programmers to develop a new compiler for every program they write.

> **We do not count use of high-level languages as reuse.**

The second issue makes us ask if we should differentiate between the relative powers of programming languages. Third- and fourth-generation languages have far more expressive power (and corresponding benefit) than assembler languages [69]. Do we attribute more reuse to people who use more powerful languages even if, for example, some programmers must work in assembler for performance or other reasons? Applications that use a combination of languages exacerbate the problem. We could convert all languages to a common unit such as *equivalent assembler instructions* or *function points* using a process Capers Jones calls "backfiring" [71]. However, this adds expense and additional margin for error in our data collection.

We do not distinguish between different generations of programming languages for purely practical reasons. Therefore, reusing a line of code in one language counts the same as reusing a line of code in any other language. If we could collect actual data on *effort*, then perhaps we could get a more accurate picture of the benefits of reuse, not only across languages, but also across software work products and life-cycle phases. Chapter 9, "Measuring Reuse Across the Life Cycle," presents a method to address measuring reuse of all software workproducts. Meanwhile, we do not recommend special reuse allowances based on programming language.

USE OF TOOLS

Does use of text editors, debuggers, test drivers, and configuration management systems mean we "reuse" the source code of these tools? Programmers use tools because they make the job easier; we do not expect to write new tools every time we write a new program.

> ### We do not count the use of tools as reuse.

The author once had a lively discussion with someone who insisted that when we used the compiler tools Lex and Yacc, we should count the source code of these tools as reuse [68, 83]. When Lex and Yacc first arrived in the programming world, we might both have agreed. However, Lex and Yacc have since achieved a status that puts them more into the category of "tools" than of "reusable software." Consequently, we do not consider the use of these or similar tools as reuse. They do, however, serve as another good example of how our views of reuse change as our expectations mature. We will discuss how we count the *output* of these and other code generating tools in "Application Generators" on page 44.

USE VERSUS REUSE OF COMPONENTS

Does every *use* of a component count as a "reuse" of the component? This point confuses and distorts more experience reports than any other. The confusion comes from having to differentiate between basic programming practices and reuse practices that lead to a quantifiable savings. The following example illustrates this difference.

A use versus reuse example

One site which developed communications software for IBM's mainframe operating systems reported 11K LOC of reuse on a relatively small component. When examining the numbers from the metrics database, we found that 5120 lines of this reuse came from one 10-line reusable macro. Furthermore, all 5120 lines came from *the same module*. This particular module had the function of placing one page of data on a serial bus one character at a time. It did this by using the reusable macro *transmit character (XMIT_CH)*. With a page size of 512 bytes, the original code read:

```
Do i := 1 to 512
         XMIT_CH(i);
```

We normally would count this as 2 source instructions (one for the "Do ... while" and one for the call to XMIT_CH) and 10 reused instructions (which make up macro XMIT_CH). However, because communications systems require exceptionally high performance, the programmer performed a common optimization technique called "unrolling the loop."[6] This resulted in the following source code:

```
XMIT_CH(1);
XMIT_CH(2);
XMIT_CH(3);
XMIT_CH(4);
XMIT_CH(5);
XMIT_CH(6);

      .
      .
      .

XMIT_CH(509);
XMIT_CH(510);
XMIT_CH(511);
XMIT_CH(512);
```

The programmer reported having written 512 source instructions and having reused 5120 instructions. The programmer reported a benefit to the project (at $100/line)[7] of approximately $50,000!

> ### We only count the first use of a component as reuse.

USE OF COMMERCIAL OFF-THE-SHELF SOFTWARE

Does use of commercial off-the-shelf (COTS) software constitute reuse? In other words, if we store data in a database system, does this mean we "reused" the source code of the database? Does building a spreadsheet mean we "reuse" the source code of the spreadsheet product? No known company counts the use of these *prerequisite products* in any of its software metrics, because they do not consider the database or spreadsheet part of the application developed for the customer. For the same reason, we do not consider these products "reused."

> ### We do not count COTS products as reuse.

---

[6] Unrolling a loop removes the need to do three things on every iteration: (1) test to see if the loop counter *i* equals the termination condition, (2) increment the loop counter, and (3) execute the branch back to the beginning of the loop.

[7] The examples in this book use an industry average software development cost of $100 per LOC [52].

With that said, we need to look closer at COTS products and the three different ways that they affect software development.

1. COTS we deliver as *complete applications*, such as word processors, checkbook managers, or inventory control systems. These complete applications often come "shrink-wrapped" and ready-to-use. We do not count them as reuse, even when we may integrate the product into a larger application.

2. COTS we specify as *prerequisite products*, such as databases or spreadsheets. We usually build applications with these products either using proprietary languages that come with the product, or using standard programming languages (i.e., Ada, C, C++) that access the product via bindings or Application Programming Interfaces (APIs). We do not count prerequisite products as reuse.

3. COTS *parts libraries* such as class libraries or commercial abstract data type collections [19]. Buying parts can be a cheaper alternative to building reusable components, especially for domain-independent software, as discussed in "Expected Levels of Reuse" on page 5. We count the use of these components as reuse and account for the purchase costs or license fees of these components in our economic models as appropriate.

The use of COTS products versus building a custom application comes down to a basic "build or buy" decision. If we can find a suitable existing shrink-wrapped application, it will almost always cost significantly less to buy it than to develop one ourselves. We also save money by placing the responsibility for technical support and maintenance on the organization that developed the COTS product. However, we lose much of our ability to customize the product, and we often tie ourselves to some manufacturer's proprietary standards. The decision to use COTS products or to take a COTS integration approach to software development must come after considering these and other issues.

PORTED SOFTWARE

In many cases, organizations write applications to run on several platforms. In these cases, the porting process usually consists of simply recompiling the software for each platform, perhaps after making minor configuration changes of certain environmental variables. Do we count this recompilation for a different target platform as "reuse"?

A porting example

A project for the U.S. Navy involved developed a large software system for use on a family of embedded systems for the Restructured Navy Tactical Data System

(RNTDS). The software had to allow for a set of customized variables for specific weapons, guidance, and navigation. Once the embedded systems were configured, the Navy compiled and loaded the same software on each. Subsequent reports showed reuse levels of 99.9% for each embedded system fielded. These consistent "reuse" levels of 99.9% led to cost reductions from the original $9,084/unit down to $310/unit [135].

This example shows how an organization can distort reuse metrics by counting porting as reuse. We cannot compare the productivity rates of porting code with new development. To prevent situations like that above, organizations should report porting separately in their software metrics.

> **We do not count porting as reuse.**

APPLICATION GENERATORS

Do we count code generated by application generators as "reuse"? This category is an example of something we really want our developers to do, but that also can greatly distort all of our software metrics, especially productivity and reuse. We simply cannot compare the output of these tools with that of programmers who write software one line at a time.

> **We do not count generated code as reuse.**

An application generator example

In a project for the U.S. Army, a team of three programmers worked for two months on a rapid-prototype front end to a database application. Most of the application consisted of the Graphical User Interface (GUI) that they generated using a commercial WYSIWYG forms tool; they physically wrote about 4K LOC of scripts and C code to tie the forms together. The final prototype consisted of 103K LOC of C, which the project manager reported as 99% reuse with a productivity rate of 17K LOC per programmer-month.

To encourage the use of application generators without distorting the metrics as shown above, we recommend reporting generated code separately from other code. Assume the prototype obtained 500 LOC from a government reuse library. In this case, the software reuse report might sound like this: "We delivered 104K LOC of C, of which we generated 99K LOC using a GUI forms tool. Of the 4K LOC we wrote, we obtained 500 LOC from external sources. This resulted in a reuse level of: 500 LOC ÷ 4,000 LOC = 12.5 % .”

CODE LIBRARIES

We have reached a point in our spectrum of software categories where we will soon have to draw the line between good programming, expected practices, and what we want to count as reuse. Exactly where an organization draws this line will depend somewhat on the organization and culture as they relate to the guidelines that follow.

Use of utility libraries

Utility libraries consist of software that essentially belongs to the programming language. The input/output library *stdio* in C provides a good example; we cannot do much in C without it. Everyone must use *stdio*, and we do not count it as reuse. Basic math functions also fall into this category; in languages such as C and Ada the programmer has to explicitly include the math library to use it; however, we do not count the use of included functions such as *square_root* as reuse.

> **We do not count software from utility libraries as reuse.**

Use of local utility libraries

An organization may have local utility libraries which it *expects or requires* all programmers to use. At the IBM Mid-Hudson Valley Programming Laboratory (MHVPL), where they develop the Multiple Virtual Storage (MVS)[8] operating system, nearly every programmer uses the memory request macro GETMAIN; they could not do their jobs without it. However, there exist other kinds of utilities that do not have such a clear-cut, universal role. An organization may elect to count software from these local utility libraries as reuse, depending on the nature of the software and the local programming environment.

> **We may count software from utility libraries as reuse.**

Project- and domain-specific libraries

When organizations engineer collections of software for repeated use within an application area we call the collection a project or domain-specific library. Reuse metrics should encourage the development of domain-specific libraries, because experiences across industry show that high levels of reuse virtually require this kind of software.

---

[8] Trademark of the International Business Machines Corporation.

> **We count software from project- and domain-specific libraries as reuse.**

Corporate reuse libraries

Finally, the corporation may explicitly supply reusable collections of domain-independent, general-purpose software such as abstract data types (ADTs), container classes, and GUI objects. The use of this software counts as reuse.

> **We count software from reuse libraries as reuse.**

USE OF MODIFIED SOFTWARE

The discussion up to this point has focused on "black-box" reuse, or the use of unmodified software. However, "white-box" reuse, or copying and modifying existing software, also has many benefits. How does modifying software affect reuse levels and expected benefits?

Black-box reuse provides a major benefit not only during development, but also during maintenance. In fact, the maintenance savings of black-box reuse can greatly exceed those obtained during development [127]. One estimate shows that maintenance savings alone with black-box reuse can yield 8–10 times the development costs in ROI [72]. This provides a cogent argument for encouraging black-box reuse.

White-box reuse provides less of a benefit during development because the programmer has to make and test the modifications. Furthermore, these benefits do not extend past the development phase of the life cycle. Every time a programmer copies and modifies a piece of software the programmer contributes to the maintenance costs of the organization. Figure 5 emphasizes how a small near-term temptation can contribute to a significant long-term cost. With 60–80% of the life cycle consisting of maintenance, we really want to encourage black-box reuse.

Hewlett-Packard collected data on more than 200 software projects from 1981 to 1989 and found that components that projects reused without modification had one-third to one-tenth the defect density of new software [58]. This high quality contributed to significant maintenance savings as long as the projects practiced black-box reuse. Modifying the components resulted in software with no improvement in error density compared to new software.

Other studies confirm the findings at Hewlett-Packard. For example, Thomas *et al.* at the University of Maryland give four classes of software relative to reuse [138]:

1. New

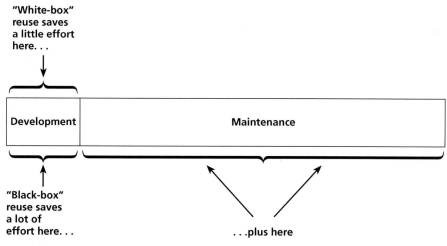

"White-box" reuse saves a little effort here. . .

Development	Maintenance

"Black-box" reuse saves a lot of effort here. . .

. . .plus here

FIGURE 5 *White-box versus black-box reuse. The benefits of reusing without modification dwarf those obtainable by modifying the software.*

2. Extensive modification (>25% modified)
3. Slight modification (<25% modified)
4. Verbatim

Their study also showed that verbatim reuse resulted in 10 times less error density than new or extensively modified software. The study further showed that new and extensively modified components tend to have about the same error densities. This confirms the evidence that making many modifications to components practically erases the long-term benefit of reuse. Therefore:

> **We do not count modified components as reuse.**

This does not mean that we do not receive benefits from white-box reuse. It just means that systematic reuse programs encourage reusing software without change because of the superior benefits they receive from black-box reuse throughout the life cycle. In fact, several reuse metric models include some measure for white-box reuse. For example, the DISA metrics track white-box as well as black-box reuse [34].[9]

---

[9] The DISA reuse metrics track *adaptive reuse* (white-box reuse) separately from *verbatim reuse* (black-box reuse) and report it as a separate line item for tracking cost avoidance benefit. However, the adaptive reuse does not contribute to the reuse level of the product. See "Defense Information Systems Agency: Reuse Metrics and ROI" on page 83.

The difference in benefits justifies this decision, but there are also more practical reasons. Although a programmer may obtain a significant development benefit from copying and modifying only 1 line of a 1K LOC component, the data most organizations collect cannot differentiate this component from one in which the programmer modified 50% or more of the code. This makes it impractical to assign values to the development benefits gained from partially modified components.

Finally, the IEEE Standard for Software Productivity Metrics defines "reuse" as the number of source statements incorporated *without modification* into an application system [64]. According to the IEEE standard, new or *changed* source statements count as new software. Modifying software for use in new applications falls into the field of *reengineering*.

❖ APPLYING THE COUNTING RULES TO OBJECT-ORIENTED SOFTWARE

Recent articles and publications cite reuse as a principal benefit of object-oriented technology; however, object-oriented projects face the same issues as any other development project when it comes to defining what to count as "reused" software. Experience reports from OO projects routinely state impressive reuse levels and benefits due to reuse. However, we cannot trust these reports without understanding what the reports counted: e.g., inheritance or polymorphism. As with most experience reports, recent work in OO metrics fails to address this issue. Part of the problem comes from counting "internal" reuse in OO reuse metrics: in other words, using your own code [49, 75, 137]. This common and unfortunate misconception within the OO community really confuses many unwary practitioners. Another part of the problem with OO metrics work comes from counting modified software as reuse.

A recent survey of 300 European UNIX and object-oriented software developers showed that they adopted OO technology to take advantage of object reuse [145]. The survey found that 37% of 300 companies had software reuse as their primary goal, with 33% looking for better-quality code and 29% hoping for faster development times. To accomplish this, one-third of the companies invested heavily in OO, with 90% of those choosing C++. However, many of these companies (24% of the total) count as the simple cutting and pasting of code as reuse. This reveals one reason why so many OO projects claim such high reuse levels. Furthermore, only 9% of the surveyed companies currently have a systematic reuse program in place. This brings into question how these companies control their reusable software and whether they consistently apply reuse metrics to their projects.

To illustrate the problem of measuring software reuse in OO development, Kain notes the limited availability of quantitative evidence of reuse in object-oriented programming and observes that few experience reports say how they measure reuse [72]. Kain cites evidence that some reports count reuse as the use of classes and methods across applications (as explained in "The Boundary Problem" on page 34) and not, for example, inheritance within an application. Other reports count inheritance as reuse of the superclass. As we have seen, these differences in how to count prevent the comparison of OO experience reports.

Although Kain recognizes the need to evaluate OO reuse in the context of multiple teams and organizations (not individual programmers), another interpretation comes from Henderson-Sellers. He claims reuse comes from subclassing via inheritance and from multiple instantiations of the same class [59]. Although he focuses on the reuse of classes from reusable class libraries, Henderson-Sellers includes references to the reuse of classes from one project to another and from classes built for reuse within the organization. These different attitudes about what constitutes OO reuse confuse and distort experience reports just as they do in the procedural paradigm. Henderson-Sellers discusses reuse economics using the cost–benefit model presented in Chapter 5.

The issues surrounding the *boundary problem* primarily determine whether to count OO software as "reused." In addition to considering whether an organization saved effort by obtaining classes from other sources, we need to determine whether the organization used the software with (*white-box*) or without (*black-box*) modification. In practice, uncontrolled and unplanned subclassing results in code as fragile and hard to maintain as procedural code [1]. This section clarifies the reuse counting rules with respect to objects. Although the rules discussed in this chapter apply equally to various development paradigms, this section will specifically address how they relate to object-oriented reuse metrics. In short, the rationale for the counting rules applies equally to the functional, procedural, and object-oriented paradigms because the rationale does not depend on any paradigm-specific methods [111].

REUSE IN THE OBJECT-ORIENTED PARADIGM

This section describes the three primary OO reuse methods and briefly discusses the benefits and drawbacks of each. It compares each of these methods to the analogous practice in traditional procedural development. Finally, the section presents some issues that an organization should address when instituting reuse metrics for OO development.

Expectations of high reuse levels provide one of the most important motivations for OO software development. The OO paradigm provides three primary ways to support reuse:

1. **Classes.** The encapsulation of function and data to provide for their use through multiple instantiation and in aggregation relationships with other classes.

2. **Inheritance.** The extension of a class into subclasses by specializing an abstract class or an existing class to allow subclasses to share common features.

3. **Polymorphism.** The reduction of program complexity by providing the same operation on several data types via several implementations for a common interface.

Each of these reuse approaches involves some trade-offs in terms of application and desirability. These trade-offs include the "cleanliness" of the reuse: in other words, whether or not each component has a traceable heritage of evolution, and consequently whether or not changes to a component will result in changes throughout the system [30]. For example, creating a subclass and overloading a method through polymorphism can cause unexpected results at execution time if there is a name conflict between the methods. Modifying source code, whether for the method implementation or simply for the interface, will propagate changes to all parts of the system using that method. Alternatively, simple subclassing (without polymorphism) or use of a method without modification of source code provides for clean and safe reuse.

This view of OO reuse takes into account the subsequent testing made necessary by inheritance and polymorphism [14]. For testing purposes, each inherited method requires retesting, and each possible binding of a polymorphic component requires a separate test. Again, the extent of testing required depends on the "cleanliness" of the reuse, just as the extent of testing in procedural languages depends on the modifications to the implementation or interface of the component.

If OO language features do not guarantee reuse, they certainly do not guarantee good programming [55]. In traditional procedural development, programmers use language features such as macros, functions, and procedures when they repeatedly execute the same operations. The programmer may use techniques (depending on the implementation language) such as variable macros (a method for overloading macro definitions), generic packages (a method for overloading abstract data types in Ada), or parameterized functions (a method for passing logic into a routine through the routine's interface). We consider the use of these language features and techniques "good programming" or "good design." Likewise, we expect OO programmers to use the language features at their disposal (e.g., subclassing, inheritance, and polymorphism) to abstract features common to objects and to minimize the amount of code they write and maintain.

Recall that in traditional development, we consider a component "reused" when the programmer avoided writing it by obtaining it from "someplace else." Within small teams or organizations, we expect the use of macros, functions, and procedures for common functions. Repeated calls to these components do not count as reuse; calling components simply *uses* the features of procedural languages. However, if the organization obtains the software from another organization or product, we count it as reuse.

Likewise, a small team or organization may build a class hierarchy in which subclasses incrementally specialize the common aspects of an abstract class or define the implementations of deferred classes. We expect subclassing, inheritance, and polymorphism in OO development. Of course, multiple instantiations of an object do not count as reuse for the same reason multiple calls to a function do not count. Reuse in OO programs comes from the use of classes and methods obtained from other organizations or products, thereby resulting in a savings of development effort.

Determining when an organization has saved effort by using OO software means considering the issues discussed in "The Boundary Problem" on page 34. As with procedural development, boundaries on OO projects are obvious from the structure of the organization (the people) and/or the structure of the software. In most cases management structure maps to the software structure. On small projects, "reused" classes come from preexisting class libraries, commercially licensed class libraries, or other projects. On large projects, the many organizations working on the project will reuse each other's classes as well as software from other external sources. On large projects with a systematic reuse program, organizations will often use software developed for reuse *by a team dedicated to building and supporting shared classes.*

MEASURING REUSE LEVELS FOR OBJECT-ORIENTED DEVELOPMENT

The definition of reuse and what should count as a *Reused Source Instruction (RSI)* (or reused objects) applies to all programming paradigms. The use of language features such as functions, procedures, generics, and (variable) macros in the procedural paradigm, or classes, inheritance, and polymorphism in the OO paradigm do not, by themselves, constitute "reuse" as much as they represent a particular method of solving a problem.

> *The rationale for defining reuse in any paradigm depends not on language features, but rather on whether someone saved effort by using software they obtained from someplace else.*

The solution to determining reuse levels in programs lies in the *boundary problem*. We expect organizations to call procedures and inherit methods that the organization developed for its own use. When an organization avoided development by using

TABLE 10　*Summary: Measuring OO Reuse across Boundaries*

Types of reuse	Measured?
Subclassing, with polymorphism	No
Subclassing, without polymorphism	Yes
Object composition	Yes
Parameterized types	Yes

software it obtained from someplace else, then we say it "reused" the software. As OO metrics mature and the community identifies the most meaningful metrics and ranges of values for each, the metrics must include consistent definitions of reuse to serve as a basis for comparing results.

In conclusion, when analyzing OO software for reuse, we use the same rationale as for any other programming paradigm. Benefits vary depending on whether we do subclassing, composition, or polymorphism. Normally, the difference in the benefits shows up in the maintenance phase: do we add to the maintenance trail by producing another "copy of the code"? The difference between "black-box" and "white-box" reuse in OO depends on the modification we make in the object's behavior and the amount of testing required to prove how well we did the modification. OO has a unique feature in that it allows us to control modifications to a parent class but still change its behavior. This shows up as additional testing: do we need to retest the behavior of the parent class? Table 10 summarizes how modifications propagate throughout OO programs and subsequently affect testing. Of course, counting reuse in OO depends primarily on whether the organizations developed the classes for its own use or obtained the classes from another organization or project.

❖ COMMON QUESTIONS ABOUT WHAT TO COUNT

Having a clear definition of "reuse" makes all the difference in a reuse metrics program. In focusing on the definition, the organization will ultimately benefit. The definition ensures that the metric values accurately reflect reuse trends, because the organization will measure the same way each time it collects the metrics. The model adds credibility to cost avoidance and ROI analysis, because managers can see what does and what does not contribute to the benefits. Most importantly, having a well-understood set of counting rules brings a sense of *equity* to all the groups subject to the rules. Without rules, development teams will attempt to use the metrics to their advantage. This leads to the complete breakdown of a software metrics program.

No matter how well the counting rules define RSI, we will face questions and unusual situations that require an interpretation of the rules. In these cases, we must return to the principle:

> **Would the organization have had to develop the component if they had not obtained it from someplace else?**

In that sense, does the organization benefit from the (re)use of the component? This principle can help address most counting issues. In addition, we will answer the following questions, which commonly arise when implementing a reuse metric program:

1. How do we count unreachable code?
2. How do we count unused code in a reused component?
3. What about performance penalties caused by this unused code?
4. What if we don't use LOC?
5. How do we count new versions?
6. How do we count reused components that reuse other components?
7. Can cutting and pasting count as reuse, too?
8. What happens when reusable software changes?
9. How do we count the reuse of two similar components?
10. When does an organization count code it developed as reuse?

1. How do we count unreachable code?

Unreachable code may inflate reported reuse levels. Most code metrics we use come from commercial lines-of-code counting tools. To identify this situation, the line-counting tool would have to generate call graphs to make sure that all lines, subroutines, or modules actually connect to the "main program" in the call graph. This situation could occur in at least four ways:

1. Extraneous lines remaining in the source code for the purpose of testing or debugging. We could argue that the developer had to write this code in order to complete the module and that it should count as reuse. Another convincing argument stems from the realization that we do not generally have a practical means to filter out these lines when gathering our data. We recommend counting these lines as reuse for these reasons.

2. A mistake or error in the code. In this case, the test organization should identify and delete the unreachable code and it does not count as reuse.

3. On purpose, in order to run up the reuse level and "look good." People can always figure out a way to lie with numbers; metrics should not police people's behavior. However, in reality this situation does not often occur because other constraints, such as memory size, do not allow the inclusion of excess software.

4. By inclusion of an entire reusable class library/generic package that happens to contain unneeded member functions/procedures (e.g., include an entire queue library even though the application never calls the *isempty* function). Take the case of a reused class *stack*, which contains numerous methods for testing the status of and manipulating the stack. However, a developer may only need the *push* and *pop* methods. Do we count reuse based on code used by the developer (*push*, *pop*), or total code in the reused *stack* class?

In this case we count reuse based on the entire library, and not just the used functions, for three reasons:

a. The lack of evidence that this would greatly affect the numbers, on average.
b. The difficulty of data collection.
c. It encourages black-box reuse, e.g., of an abstract data type.

Strictly speaking, reuse should include only lines actually used (accessible in the call graph). We base our suggested approach of counting the entire library on the combination of practical considerations above.

2. How do we count unused code in a reused component?

This question involves counting "extra" code within a reused class or component. Generalizing a component may require additional code. Take the case of a variable macro instantiation. Do we count reuse based on:

1. The code produced in that instantiation,

2. The average code produced over all possible instantiations,

3. The maximum code produced of all possible instantiations,

4. The macro source code needed for that instantiation, including error checking on input parameters and environment variables, or

5. The total macro source, to include code for all possible macro instantiations and the error checking for each—in which case we may attribute reuse for a significant amount of software the programmer would not have written?

Generalizing objects may require additional code to support many possible applications. In practice, constraints (such as on object code size) restrict the ability to include more code than a developer needs. In addition to encouraging the use of preexisting classes and components, this realization supports counting the entire class or component rather than trying to determine the subset of code actually used.

3. What about performance penalties caused by this unused code?

We have seen many anecdotes but very little quantitative data to support the notion that reusable code does not perform as well as custom code. Although we all know that overconfigurability and generalization can adversely affect performance, real-world constraints exist to keep these under control. For example, using variable macro expansions and optimizing compilers can reduce the actual space and time requirements needed to run any program. Of course, any quantifiable performance impact due to reuse will depend on the situation. One project at Lockheed Martin Federal Systems estimated an increase in load module size of 15–25% due to configuration options embedded in their software. However, the same team reported little or no increase in execution overhead [9].

4. What if we don't use LOC?

We need to work with available or easily obtainable data during data collection in order to keep costs low and to avoid influencing metric values. For reuse metrics, we need to know the size of each reused component, the total size of the application, and the developers and users of each component. Most current software metrics use "lines of code" for measuring component size; this measure gives an excellent indication of overall effort. Other measures of effort may include function points, the total number of classes or objects, and the total number of methods.

As an example of using other units, consider increasing the granularity of the units to objects, procedures, functions, or configuration items. In these cases, we would report reuse level (for example) as "percent of objects reused." Measuring the "percent of objects reused" makes sense especially if all objects in the system represent about the same amount of code, information, or effort. However, when reused components vary greatly in size, this metric can result in a net loss of information and potentially misleading results—for example, because we end up giving the same value to reusing a 5 LOC object as we do to reusing a 5000 LOC object.

Example 1: When conducting a study of reusable objects on a major project, Lockheed Martin Federal Systems observed that 52% of their Ada reusable objects possessed a particular type of design documentation intended to help developers reuse the objects. Upon hearing this, personnel familiar with the reusable objects questioned the quantitative evidence that "over half of the objects" had the documentation. After further analysis using lines of code, they discovered that only 17.5% of the code had the associated detailed designs. Although "over half" the objects had the design documentation, they consisted of only the smallest reusable objects.

Example 2: AT&T Bell Labs conducted a reuse study of a large communications software project written in the C language [27]. The project reuses software from the Advance Software Technology (AST) collection of software utilities that about a dozen developers wrote for platform-independent reuse across AT&T. As part of their analysis, the AT&T researchers calculated reuse levels for various commands developed by the project, using units of (1) *C functions* and (2) LOC. Table 11 shows how much the reuse levels for each command varied depending on the unit used. The levels often varied by a factor between 2 and 3; on the *create* command the reuse level calculated using functions ended up over *8 times higher* than the reuse level calculated using LOC!

In general, using lines of code avoids pitfalls due to object size. Other units will work, especially when the units always have approximately equal size. However, when an application contains objects of varying size, the most reliable reuse levels will result from metrics that have some way to account for the variations.

5. How do we count new versions?

In the list of what an organization should and what they should not count as reuse, we say that Version 2.5 of an application does not "reuse" Version 2.4. Organizations normally base all software metrics (including reuse) on the new or changed code in V2.5. Take the example where V2.4 contains 100K LOC. Assume that V2.5 does not touch 90K LOC of that, but modifies 10K LOC for various reasons. On top of that 10K LOC, V2.5 includes an additional 20K LOC of new code. In this example, we

TABLE 11   *Reuse Levels at AT&T as Measured by C Function and LOC*

Reusing command	Reuse level measured using functions	Reuse level measured using LOC
audit	17.2%	57.9%
create	3.3%	0.4%
delete	9.8%	17.1%
gen	8.2%	8.0%
query	48.8%	88.5%
export	25.0%	63.5%

base all metrics on 10+20K LOC. To measure the reuse level of V2.5, we determine how much of the 30K LOC was reused from sources external to V2.4.

6. How do we count reused components that reuse other components?

Sometimes reusing a component results in that component, in turn, making use of other components. Do we also count those components in our reuse levels? We say "yes," subject to rules regarding boundaries and counting a component only once.

Refer to Figure 6. The figure shows a new application that reuses a software component, *R*, that it obtained from "someplace else." In order to function, component *R* uses software components *A*, *B*, and *C*. We therefore count these components as reused. The figure also shows that components *B* and *C* both use component *D*. We count component *D* as reused one time.

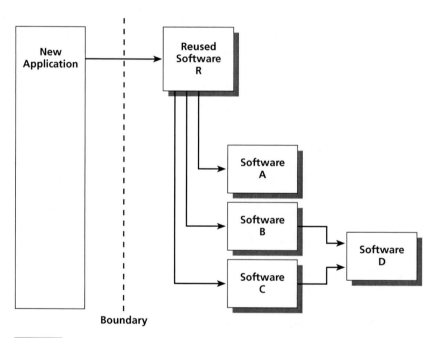

FIGURE 6 *Counting Software Used by Reused Software*

As always, the rationale applies to all programming paradigms, to include OO. In OO applications, all code in the inheritance hierarchy counts as reused code subject to the boundary problem and one use only. The arrows representing component "uses" in Figure 6 represent inheritance, procedure calls, included software, etc.

7. Can cutting and pasting count as reuse, too?

"Cutting and pasting" means modifying software by using portions of a preexisting program. Quickly grabbing code with the mouse and dropping it into a new program can make a developer more productive. However, the definition of reuse presented in this chapter asserts that we should only count black-box reuse. This agrees with the IEEE definition. Review the evidence in "Use of Modified Software" on page 46. Although this type of white-box reuse has benefits, the much greater benefits of black-box reuse, especially in the maintenance phase, makes it the only really consequential definition for use in economic models.

8. What happens when reusable software changes?

If we do not count modified components, then whenever we have to change a "reusable" component we do not count that component as reused. This could happen if we need to adapt an existing reusable component for a new, unforeseen requirement. It could also happen if we found a reusable component with a function that "almost" does what we need. If an organization finds reusable software and they modify that software, they will have to retest, redocument, and maintain that software from that point forward. We do not count this as reuse.

However, some organizations have dedicated reuse development teams for the purpose of building and maintaining common code. Refer to "Reuse Development Team and Librarian" on page 94 for an example organization. In these situations, the reuse team must take special care during requirements analysis and design to allow for the needs of all expected reusers. Configuration management of the reused software becomes critical because any change to the fielded software will affect everyone who reuses it.

On occasion, new requirements will emerge that require modifications to the reusable software. However, the responsibility for making the modifications and maintaining the software still lies with the reuse development team and not the reusing organizations. As this software "evolves," we still count its use as reuse.

9. How do we count the reuse of two similar components?

Consider the situation where many departments contribute to a very large project. We consider a component reused when a department obtains a component from another department that works on the project or when it obtains a component from any source outside the project. Department A obtains a component C from the corporate reuse repository and uses it in their code. Now Department B needs a component to perform a virtually identical function to C. Unaware of the work done by Department A, Department B searches for and obtains a component C′ from another project.

Even though this reveals an inefficient software development process, both departments A and B received a reuse benefit from their use of C and C′. Therefore, both departments should count the use of their components as reuse. If an organization becomes aware of this kind of situation, it normally would select one of C or C′ for use by both departments.

10. When does an organization count code it developed as reuse?

When an organization starts work on a new project and uses a component it developed on a previous project, the use counts as reuse on the second project, though not on the first. Of course, the rationale for our reuse counting rules applies: the organization uses the component without modification, they only count the first use, etc. In this example the organization has saved effort by using the component in a new context. Counting the component as reuse makes sense because the component crossed a *project* boundary. The figures in "The Boundary Problem: Small Projects Versus Large Projects" on page 36 show that software crossing project boundaries counts as reuse.

Consider a situation in which many organizations work on the same project. For efficiency, we want one team to build and maintain software that these organizations share. If the software may apply to other projects, then the software should go into a common repository or reuse library so that other projects have access to the reusable components. In this way only one copy of the reusable software exists. Every time an organization extracts the software from the common area and uses it, it counts as reuse. If an organization extracts a component for use on one project and then extracts the same component for use on a second project, both projects count the use of that component towards each project's reuse level.

❖ CONCLUSION

We have now completed our definition of reuse from the metrics point of view; Table 12 summarizes the conclusions.

We define:

> **Definition:** We refer to software that complies with the definition above as a *Reused Source Instruction (RSI)*.

The use of the term RSI in any equation or text indicates compliance with the specific counting method just given. Using RSI gives us a standard reference to use when evaluating reuse metric values.

TABLE 12   *Summary: What to Measure as Reuse*

Type of reuse	Measured?
Maintenance	No
Operating System	No
High-level languages	No
Tools	No
Multiple uses	One time
Commercial off the shelf (COTS) software	No
Porting	Separately
Application generators	Separately
Utility libraries	No
Local utility libraries	Maybe
Project/domain-specific libraries	Yes
Subclassing, with polymorphism	No
Subclassing, without polymorphism	Yes
Object composition	Yes
Parameterized types	Yes
Black-box	Yes
White-box	No

❖ 5 ❖

Measuring
Reuse and
Reuse Benefits

Having defined what to count, we now present different metric models. Reuse metrics have a unique role because most software reuse metrics encourage writing more code. Developers often receive awards and promotions based on their productivity. We want to *discourage* writing code, which means reuse metrics will contradict the existing programmer culture and mindset [104].

Several of the following models focus exclusively on measuring reuse level. As previously discussed, reuse percent serves as the de facto industry standard measure of reuse level. Nearly every industry experience report uses *reuse percent*. The remaining models report reuse level via a decimal ranging from 0 to 1.0. This *reuse ratio* conveys the same information without the convenience of a percent sign.

This chapter presents several major reuse metric and economic models. These models have influenced reuse metrics through their early introduction, their longevity, or their appearance in major publications:

1. Banker *et al.*: Reuse metrics
2. Frakes and Terry: Reuse level
3. Gaffney and Durek: Reuse economics
4. Balda and Gustafson: Estimation using modified COCOMO
5. Barnes and Bollinger: Cost–benefit analysis
6. Henderson-Sellers: Cost–benefit analysis
7. Malan and Wentzel: Cost–benefit analysis with NPV
8. Poulin and Caruso: Reuse metrics and ROI
9. U.S. Defense Information Systems Agency (DISA): Reuse metrics and ROI

We intend for these models to represent the approaches to reuse metrics and economics that we discussed in Chapter 2, "A Reuse Metrics Overview." We also use the models to illustrate how the original developer of the model either considered or ignored the data to input to the model. This chapter uses the same terms and lexicon as the original models, although we will often provide translations to help clarify the equations. Interested readers can consult Lim's use of a common lexicon to translate and represent reuse economic models [85].

When selecting a model to use, we first need to decide what the organization *really* wants to measure. Does the organization want to simply track reuse levels, or does it want to quantify reuse benefits, perhaps as derived from reuse level? Does the organization want estimates of payoff based on expected levels of reuse for an upcoming project? Each model has a different purpose both in goals and in what it measures.

❖ BANKER *ET AL.*: REUSE METRICS

Banker *et al.*, implemented a set of metrics in a repository-based CASE environment called the High Productivity Systems (HPS) [7, 8]. They used these metrics on projects at two separate firms. However, the metrics violate several of the counting rules presented in Chapter 4, "Defining Reuse from a Metrics Point of View." We start this chapter with these metrics mostly to illustrate how the use of widely published model can result in misleading values for reuse and reuse benefits. Before using any model, we must understand how the model works.

Banker *et al.* define reuse metrics in terms of software *objects* (modules, macros, etc.) rather than lines of code. This helps enforce the difference between black-box and white-box reuse (an object with any modifications does not qualify as reused). However, as shown in the answer to question 4, "What if we don't use LOC?" on page 55, working at the object level of granularity can yield deceptive results if the objects vary greatly in size (reusing a small object counts the same as reusing a large one). This model does not have any way to account for systems that contain objects of varying size.

Using the de facto industry standard, the model measures the level of reuse using *Reuse Percentage*, where:

$$Reuse\ Percentage\ =\ \left(1 - \frac{New\ objects\ built}{Total\ objects\ used}\right) \times 100\%$$

They also define a productivity index by inverting the previous equation so that:

$$Reuse\ Leverage\ =\ \frac{Total\ objects\ used}{New\ objects\ built}$$

Notice a couple of key things. First, these metrics count multiple *uses* of the same object. In the case of the macro XMIT_CH in the "use versus reuse" example in Chapter 4,

XMIT_CH would count 512 times in this equation. Second, while Banker discusses the difference between *internal reuse* and *external reuse*, the equation for *Reuse Percentage* includes both, thereby disregarding the boundary problem.

The following example shows how an organization would use these metrics. Suppose a system consists of 400 *uses* of objects, 100 objects of which programmers in the organization actually wrote. (Note that this does not necessarily mean the system contains 400 *unique* objects; it may actually contain just the 100 newly created objects, some of which the system uses many times). The *Reuse Percentage* equals:

$$Reuse\ Percentage\ =\ \left(1 - \frac{100\ Objects}{400\ Objects}\right) \times 100\% = 75\%$$

The *Reuse Leverage* equals:

$$Reuse\ Leverage\ =\ \frac{400\ Objects}{100\ Objects} = 4$$

Because this model counts multiple uses of objects as multiple instances of reuse, the *Reuse Percentage* metric could mean many things. For example, if the system contains many calls to the 100 objects developed specifically for this application, then we would say the reuse level really equals zero. On the other hand, if the system contains only one call to every object in the system, then by our definition the reuse level could equal as much as the 75% reflected in the metric. Regarding the second metric, a *Reuse Leverage* = 4 means that the application uses, or calls, each object an average of four times. Unfortunately, this does not help interpret the meaning of the Reuse Percentage metric. Because of these anomalies, the Banker metrics serve mostly as an example of the confusion and misperceptions a reuse metric can create.

❖ FRAKES AND TERRY: REUSE LEVEL

Frakes and Terry use several reuse level metrics to measure the repeated use of functions defined within an application and the reuse of software coming from sources external to an application [45]. They call these two values the *internal reuse level* and the *external reuse level*; note that the internal reuse level metric violates our counting rules because it measures software developed within an application. Rather than use lines of code, the Frakes and Terry metrics use a software unit called *item*, meaning any function, object, or similar component. Since they did most of their work in the C programming language, an *item* usually equates to a C function. Frakes and Terry count reuse of an item subject to user selected values of the *internal threshold level (ITL)* and the *external threshold level (ETL)*.

THRESHOLD LEVELS

Threshold levels seek to *define* the maximum number of uses of a item that must occur before the use of the item counts as reuse. For example, if a threshold level is 2, then an application must call an item three times in order for the use of the item to count as reuse. Frakes and Terry define two threshold levels for a software system:

1. *External Threshold Level (ETL)*, or the maximum number of uses of an item obtained from outside the software system that can occur before its next use counts as reuse. The ETL helps determine the level of *external reuse.*

2. *Internal Threshold Level (ITL)*, or the maximum number of uses of an item within the software system that must occur before its next use counts as reuse. The ITL helps determine the level of *internal reuse.*

Three other values complete the metrics:

> *IU*, the number of items used more than the ITL.
> *EU*, the number of items used more than the ETL.
> *T*, the total number of items in the system, both external and internal.

The metrics include:

> *Internal reuse level* $= IU/T$
> *External reuse level* $= EU/T$
> *Total reuse level* $= (IU + EU)/T$

Each reuse level assumes a value between 0 and 1, inclusive, with 0 occurring in the situation of no reuse. Each item counts only one time towards the total reuse level, but in order to count the application must make at least *ITL* or *ETL* calls to the item.

Threshold levels depend solely on software structure and the values we choose to assign. They do not depend on organizational structure, as discussed in "The Boundary Problem" on page 34. Because we can vary the values of the ETL and ITL, the value for reuse level can vary. Frakes and Terry do not provide guidance as to appropriate values for ETL and ITL. Given our definition of RSI, we should always set ITL $= \infty$, so we do not count the calls to our own items as reuse, and we should set ETL $= 0$, so that the first use of an external item counts as reuse.

ACCOUNTING FOR ITEM SIZES

Recall from question 4, "What if we don't use LOC?" on page 55, that reuse metrics must account for variability in the size of reused objects or else possibly yield misleading results. Because *items* can vary in size, the Frakes and Terry metrics provide the option for *complexity weighting.*[10] Complexity weighting allows us to adapt the metrics to adjust for reusing large and small items. Using this option, the metrics remain unchanged except for multiplying each item in the system by its size, in lines of code. For example, the *total reuse level* metric when weighted for item size yields a value between 0 and 1 and represents the fraction of internal reused lines of code plus the fraction of external reused lines of code, subject to the values of ITL and ETL. In other words, it gives a level of reuse based on LOC rather than one based on items. To avoid misleading metric values, we should always use the Frakes and Terry metrics with the adjustment for "complexity."

Example: Figure 7 depicts a small C program in which the main program calls five functions. As shown by the boundary, function A and function B come from an external source, such as a reuse library. The developer of this program wrote the remaining functions C, D, and E. The figure also shows how many calls the *main* program makes to each of the functions A–E. We want to calculate the reuse level of this program.

We first decide to set the threshold levels so that $ITL = \infty$ and $ETL = 0$. to comply with our definition of RSI. We also decide to calculate the reuse level using *items* as

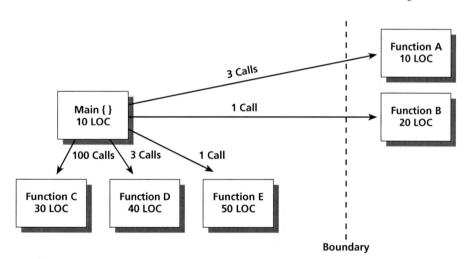

FIGURE 7 *An example C program. The program makes calls to three internal functions and two external functions.*

---

[10] The use of the term "complexity" does not mean the same as when referring to complexity metrics such as the McCabe or Halstead metrics.

well as to calculate the reuse level with LOC using the complexity weighting. Examining the figure allows us to fill in Table 13. Since we set $ITL = \infty$, the number of calls to functions C–E will never exceed ITL, so $IU = 0$. Since $ETL = 0$, the number of calls to both function A and function B exceeds ETL, so $EU = 2$. We have a total number of functions $T = 5$.

TABLE 13   *Frakes and Terry Reuse Level Data for Example C Program*

Data	By item	By LOC
IU	0	0 LOC
EU	2	30 LOC
T	5	150 LOC
Internal reuse level	0/5	0/150 LOC
External reuse level	2/5	30/150 LOC
Total reuse level	**0.4**	**0.2**

NOTE: Threshold levels: $ITL = \infty$; $ETL = 0$.

The reuse level for the program either equals 0.4 or 0.2, depending on whether we report reuse based on *items* or by LOC. Note that the reuse level will also vary based on our choice of threshold levels. For example, if we set $ITL = 2$ and $ETL = 1$, then function B would no longer count as reuse, but function C and function D would count. This results in reuse levels of either *0.6* or *0.53*, as shown in Table 14.

TABLE 14   *Varying Threshold Levels on Example C Program*

Data	By item	By LOC
IU	2	70 LOC
EU	1	10 LOC
T	5	150 LOC
Internal reuse level	2/5	70/150 LOC
External reuse level	1/5	10/150 LOC
Total reuse level	**0.6**	**0.53**

NOTE: Threshold levels: $ITL = 2$; $ETL = 1$.

Like Banker, Frakes and Terry include metrics to indicate whether most of the calls to items in a system go to internal software or to external software. This indicates *how* a program uses items (e.g., mostly through calls to items within the program static structure or mostly to calls outside the structure), as well as *how much* a program uses items. To calculate the metrics we need three additional values:

IUF, the number of references to items used more than the ITL.

EUF, the number of references to items used more than the ETL.

TF, the total number of references to items in the system (subject to ITL and ETL), both external and internal.

The metrics include:

Internal reuse frequency = IUF/TF
External reuse frequency = EUF/TF
Total reuse frequency = (IUF + EUF)/TF

The values of the frequency metrics tell us the average number of calls an application makes to its own items and the average number of calls the application makes to items it obtained from someplace else. As with their other metrics, these metrics assume values between 0 and 1, inclusive. Note that the total reuse frequency will only equal 1 if both threshold levels equal 0.

The Frakes and Terry metrics have an advantage in that a tool can automatically calculate metrics for a given system. Frakes and Terry developed the *rl* tool to calculate their metrics on applications written in the C language.

❖ GAFFNEY AND DUREK: REUSE ECONOMICS

The Gaffney and Durek model approaches ROI from the point of view of "How many times do I have to reuse a component for the effort to pay off?" Their work at the Software Productivity Consortium (SPC) emphasizes amortizing the costs of reuse over an expected market of reusers [46]. Their economic analysis shows the impact of reuse relative to that obtained on a project developed from all-new code, where the cost basis equals 1. The model assumes a centrally managed repository that must recover its costs by charging a fixed sum to the first *n* projects that use a component from the repository. The relative cost to the project depends on the cost to integrate the component into their application, the cost to build the reusable component, and the number of other projects that will share the cost of building the component. In the Gaffney and Durek model, we calculate the relative cost of the project, *C*, as:

$$C = \left(b + \frac{E}{n} - 1 \right) \times R + 1$$

Where:

C = cost of software development

R = the proportion of reused code in the product ($0 \leq R \leq 1$)

b = the cost, relative to new code, of incorporating new code into the product (e.g., *RCR*)

E = the cost, relative to new code, of developing a component for reuse (e.g., RCWR)

n = the number of expected reuses

The Gaffney and Durek equation represents a kind of reuse leverage model in that it presents project costs relative to a basis of 1. They further define reuse productivity, P, as the inverse of costs so that:

$$Productivity \; = \; P \; = \; \frac{1}{C}$$

This definition of productivity conveys reuse leverage in terms of costs rather than, for example, effort. This relationship shows that if we cut our costs in half, then our productivity has doubled.

Example: Figure 8 shows a reuse economic analysis using the reuse cost metric, C, with $RCR = b = 0.2$ and $RCWR = E = 1.5$. The lines in the graph show how overall project costs decrease as reuse levels increase and the number of reuses increase. The lines show project costs based on an average of 2, 5, and 10 reuses of each reusable component. At reuse levels up to 80%, the curves show project costs dropping 40–50% from the costs without reuse if the project reuses components 5–10 times. This analysis supports making reuse investments, especially early in a project that has a large expected number of related applications.

PAYOFF THRESHOLD

In their reuse metrics, Gaffney and Durek seek to determine how many reuses an organization needs to successfully amortize the costs of reuse. To find the payoff threshold, or the number of reusers needed to break even, they use the equation:

$$Payoff\,Threshold \; = \; n_0 \; = \; \frac{E}{1 - b}$$

Table 15 shows some possible payoff thresholds and how they depend on the relative cost of reuse and the relative cost of writing software for reuse by others. The results show that the more effort it takes to write a particular reusable component, the longer it takes to pay back. Also, the more effort it takes to reuse, the longer it takes to pay back. Refer to Chapter 3, "The Relative Costs of Developing with and for Reuse." Many of the economic models discussed in the present chapter seek to determine the number of projects that must share the costs of reuse in order to recover reuse investments. This table shows that with the example values for RCR and RCWR, the number of projects required for break-even can range from slightly over one to slightly over 13. However, using the default values of RCR and RCWR determined in Chapter 3, in other words, setting $E = 1.5$ and $b = 0.20$, reuse will break even at *less than 2 reuses.*

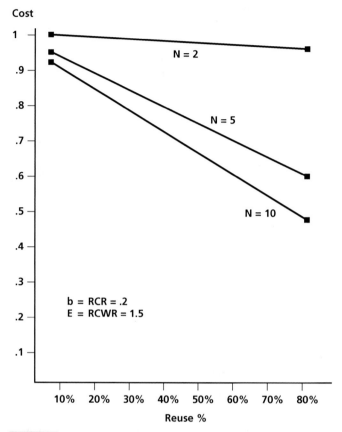

FIGURE 8 *Example Use of the Gaffney and Durek Reuse Cost Metric*

TABLE 15 *Some Possible Payoff Thresholds*

n_0 *(e.g., break-even point)*	*E (e.g., RCWR)*	*b (e.g., RCR)*
1.35	1.25	0.08
1.92	1.25	0.35
8.33	1.25	0.85
1.88	1.50	0.20
2.17	2.00	0.08
3.08	2.00	0.35
13.33	2.00	0.85

Example: You have just received an assignment to develop a series of four related applications for one of your most important customers. You have worked with the customer many times and understand the application domain very well. After a high-level design of the four applications, you determine that there exists a substantial amount of common function across the applications. You want to know if you should spend extra resources up front to develop that common function as reusable code.

You have determined from prior projects that your project has an RCR of 0.2 and an RCWR of 1.8. With this information you can use the payoff threshold to see if you should build the reusable code. Using $RCR = b = 0.2$ and $RCWR = E = 1.8$, calculate:

$$Payoff\ Threshold\ =\ n_0\ =\ \frac{E}{1-b}\ =\ \frac{1.8}{1-0.2}\ =\ 2.25$$

Since the four applications you have to build exceeds the *Payoff Threshold*, 2.25, you would benefit by developing the common functions as reusable software.

❖ BALDA AND GUSTAFSON: ESTIMATION USING MODIFIED COCOMO

Balda and Gustafson developed a model for estimating software project costs with reuse by modifying the popular Constructive Cost Model (COCOMO) [15]. COCOMO provides a standard life-cycle cost model to allow a user to measure and estimate the effort required in each phase of software development. However, although the COCOMO model has proven reliable in estimating software costs, the basic COCOMO model does not consider software reuse. Balda and Gustafson made modifications to COCOMO to address a software life-cycle with reuse [6].

To understand the modified model, it helps to start with an explanation of the original. COCOMO actually consists of three different formulas, each with a specific purpose. The basic formula provides a rough cost estimate before completion of the requirements phase. The intermediate formula provides a more specific estimate based on the characteristics of a specific project. Finally, the detailed formula estimates the cost for each phase while accounting for project characteristics.

All three COCOMO formulas input an initial estimate of effort in terms of thousands of delivered source instructions (*KDSI*) and output an effort estimate measured in programmer months (LM). COCOMO identifies three software complexity levels that affect the estimation model: application software, utility software, and system software. The basic model, for example, has the form:

$$LM = \alpha KDSI^{\beta}$$

where:

  LM = labor-months of effort
  α = complexity coefficient
  β = complexity exponent
  $KDSI$ = initial estimate of thousands of delivered source instructions

The values of the COCOMO coefficient and exponent depend on the three complexity levels of software. Table 16 gives the complexity coefficients, α, and complexity exponents, β, for use in the formula.

Balda and Gustafson made modifications to the COCOMO model to take into account the additional effort of developing code and information in future projects and the reduced effort of utilizing preexisting components. The hypothesized reuse cost estimation formula contains additional terms for code developed for future reuse, code developed from unchanged reused components, and code developed from modified components. The initial formula for development effort in labor-months has the form:

$$LM = \alpha_1 N_1^{\beta} + \alpha_2 N_2^{\beta} + \alpha_3 N_3^{\beta} + \alpha_4 N_4^{\beta}$$

where:

  $N_1 = KDSI$ for unique code developed
  $N_2 = KDSI$ for code developed for reuse
  $N_3 = KDSI$ from reused code
  $N_4 = KDSI$ from modified components

and the α_n terms represent the cost per KDSI for each type of code; α_1 for unique project code, α_2 for code developed for reuse, α_3 for reused code, and α_4 for modified code. The remaining parameters do not change from the basic COCOMO formula.

Balda and Gustafson simplified the formula by factoring out the α_n terms and combining them based on values of RCR and RCWR given in experience reports in the literature. The key simplifying assumption states that if $RCR = .1$ and $RCWR = 2.0$,

TABLE 16 *Basic COCOMO Formula Complexity Coefficients and Exponents*

Complexity level	Coefficient	Exponents
Application	2.4	1.05
Utility	3.0	1.12
System	3.6	1.20

then it takes 20 times more effort to build software for reuse than it takes to reuse it, so $\alpha_2 = 20\alpha_3$. Using this relationship to put everything in terms of α_1, then $\alpha_2 = 20\gamma\alpha_1$ and $\alpha_3 = \gamma\alpha_1$. The variable γ represents the relationship between the effort to develop unique code and the effort to reuse code; it probably lies in the range .0909 to .1739. This results in the final reuse estimation formula:

$$LM = \alpha N_1^{\beta} + 20y\alpha N_2^{\beta} + y\alpha N_3^{\beta}$$

where:

$N_1 = KDSI$ for unique code developed
$N_2 = KDSI$ for code developed for reuse
$N_3 = KDSI$ from reused code
α = complexity coefficient as in the basic COCOMO
β = complexity exponent as in the basic COCOMO

We can use this formula to estimate the development effort of a project that both reuses and builds software for reuse. However, we must calibrate the model with an appropriate value for γ for the model to work. Also, we reiterate that the model uses values of $RCR = 0.1$ and $RCWR = 2.0$, which differs from our default values by assuming easier reuse of components and more cost to develop reusable components.

Example: Assume an organization has to submit a proposal to develop an *application* to perform input and output processing of information for an inventory control system. The organization has analyzed the statement of work and determined that the application will total 30K LOC. However, the organization has extensive experience in the domain of inventory control and expects to reuse without modification approximately 18K LOC from previously built systems. They also have determined that they could add approximately 2K LOC of reusable software to their domain-specific collection of software and use it for the first time on this contract. The organization needs to estimate what it will cost to develop this system in order to bid on the contract.

The organization uses the values from Table 16 for the COCOMO *application* complexity coefficient $\alpha = 2.4$ and complexity exponent $\beta = 1.05$ in the formula. They select a value for $\gamma = .1324$, in the middle of the range. Because the organization plans to reuse 18K LOC and build 2K LOC for reuse, the amount of unique code they actually have to write for the application only comes to 30K LOC − 18K LOC − 2K LOC = 10K LOC. They estimate the effort needed to develop the application using:

$$\begin{aligned}
\text{LM} &= \alpha N_1^\beta + 20y\alpha N_2^\beta + y\alpha N_3^\beta \\
&= 2.4 \times 10\text{K LOC}^{1.05} + 20 \times .1324 \times 2.4 \times 2\text{K LOC}^{1.05} \\
&\quad + .1324 \times 2.4 \times 18\text{K LOC}^{1.05} \\
&= 26.9 \text{ LMs} + 13.1 \text{ LMs} + 6.6 \text{ LMs} \\
&= 46.6 \text{ LMs}
\end{aligned}$$

The total estimated effort of 46.6 labor months comes from 26.9 LMs to write the 10K LOC of unique code, 13.1 LMs to develop the 2K LOC for reuse, and 6.6 LMs to integrate the 18K LOC of reusable software from previous applications.

❖ BARNES AND BOLLINGER: COST–BENEFIT ANALYSIS

Barnes and Bollinger take a cost–benefit approach to the economics of reuse [10]. Recognizing that a good economic return depends on the ratio of outlays to payback, their model represents the quality of a reuse investment, Q, as reuse benefits, B, divided by reuse investments, R:

$$Q = \frac{B}{R}$$

Barnes and Bollinger do not give guidance as to how to gather data for their model; however, an extensive list of costs and benefits affecting B and R appears in Chapter 2, "A Reuse Metrics Overview." If $Q < 1$, then the reuse effort resulted in a net loss; if $Q > 1$, then the investment provided good returns. Recognizing that reuse depends on a cost sharing mechanism whereby an organization can amortize the costs of reuse across many projects, Barnes and Bollinger define the *net reuse benefit* as the difference between the *net cost to reuse* and the *reuse investment*. The model now expands to:

$$B = \left(\sum_{i=1}^{n} (D_i - A_i) \right) - I$$

where:

B = the net reuse benefit
D_i = the cost of the project without reuse
A_R = the net cost to reuse; the cost of the project with reuse, to include the costs to find, modify, and integrate reusable components

I = the total reuse investment; the cost of producing reusable components (generalization costs)

n = the number of projects reusing the software

The model shows reuse pays off when the net reuse benefit B is greater than 0. As with other C-B models, this model assumes we can determine or estimate the costs and benefits in the development cycle. With these values, we can find n, the number of projects necessary for the reuse investment to pay off, by simply setting $B = 0$.

❖ HENDERSON-SELLERS: COST–BENEFIT ANALYSIS

Henderson-Sellers used virtually the identical model and rationale as Barnes and Bollinger when presenting the following model to the OO community [59].

Henderson-Sellers focuses on the reuse of classes from reusable class libraries. He also refers to the reuse of classes across projects. However, Henderson-Sellers counts as reuse the repeated use of classes built for use within the organization and multiple instantiations of the same class. This violates one of our most important counting rules and will lead to distorted reuse levels. Although Henderson-Sellers does not explicitly identify a reuse level metric, he refers to reuse levels in terms of *percent*.

Henderson-Sellers developed an equation for the purpose of determining the ROI of reuse using cost–benefit data as input. As with other C-B models, he does not give guidance as to how to gather data for the model. The equation simply assigns values to the assorted costs associated with software development and determines if the costs without reuse exceed those with reuse. The equation achieves the same result as the model developed by Barnes and Bollinger:

$$R = \frac{S - (C_R + C_M + C_D + C_G)}{(C_G)} = \frac{S - C}{C_G} - 1$$

Where:

R = return on investment
S = cost of the project without reuse
C_R = cost to find reusable components
C_M = cost to modify components
C_D = cost to develop new components
C_G = cost of producing reusable components (generalization costs)

Note that Henderson-Sellers allows for white-box reuse in the preceding equation. The cost $C = (C_R + C_M + C_D + C_G)$ represents the total cost of reuse; the equation shows a savings due to reuse if $(S - C) > 0$ and shows the benefit of reuse if these savings exceed the costs of generalization, C_G. The equation seeks to find the point where the number of projects reusing software causes a positive benefit. This number, Q, can help justify a reuse investment if we can show that the number of potential reusers in the organization exceeds Q.

The total ROI experienced by Q projects results in summing the costs incurred by each project as well as the savings experienced by each project. The organization ROI equals:

$$R_Q = \frac{1}{Q} \times \sum_{q=1}^{Q} R_q$$

This expands and simplifies to:

$$R_Q = \frac{\sum_{q=1}^{Q} (S - C - C_G)_q}{\sum_{q=1}^{Q} C_{Gq}}$$

Where:

R_Q = the return on investment over Q projects
C_{Gq} = the cost of producing reusable components (generalization costs) incurred by project q

Henderson-Sellers performed his reuse metric analysis with the observation that conventional productivity metrics calculate productivity as a function such that *Effort = fn(Productivity, Size)*. In short, the more code you write, the higher your productivity. In the case of reuse we seek to increase productivity by writing less code. Therefore, a productivity ratio must account for reusing and generalizing software for reuse.

❖ MALAN AND WENTZEL: COST–BENEFIT ANALYSIS WITH NPV

Working in the center of research technology at Hewlett-Packard Labs, Malan and Wentzel also developed a cost–benefit model for reuse savings [87]. The model does not simply attribute the savings to a project to the difference between the total consumer savings and total producer costs. The equation includes factors for reuse-specific overhead and setup costs, such as the cost of installing and managing a reuse library, conducting a domain analysis, etc. As with other C-B models, they do not give guidance on how to collect this data. However, one point that differentiates the

Malan and Wentzel model from other models comes from their emphasis on the time value of money. This emphasis probably results from the Hewlett-Packard focus on reduced cycle times, which in turn reduces time-to-market, which in turn increases revenues. The basic model for net development cost savings, S, has the form:

$$S = \sum_{i=1}^{n} (C_{Ni} - C_{CRi}) - (C_{PR} + A)$$

Where:

> S = net development cost savings
> n = number of products sharing reusable components
> C_{Ni} = cost to develop product i without reuse
> C_{CRi} = cost to develop product i with reuse
> $C_{Ni} - C_{CRi}$ = expected consumer cost saved for product i
> C_{PR} = expected cost that the producer incurs in producing the reusable components
> A = reuse-specific overhead and setup costs incurred by the family of products

Malan and Wentzel estimate the number of reuses that a component may experience using a probability function. This adjusts the value of S for the fact that the existence of reusable components does not guarantee that an organization will actually use them. Allowing for this probability results in:

$$S = \sum_{i=1}^{n} (C_{Ni} - C_{CRi} \times p_i) - (C_{PR} + A)$$

Where:

> p_i = the probability that reuse instance i will occur

In their report Malan and Wentzel qualitatively discuss benefits such as these:

- Alternative use of freed scarce resources
- New product opportunities
- Product line consistency
- Specialization and centralization of expertise

Malan and Wentzel discount all cash values in the model using NPV whenever reuse instances take place over an extended time period. For investment analysis purposes, this time period may extend from one year to infinity. In high-technology areas where products become obsolete very quickly, the time period will generally last from three to five years. For large software development projects, the time period will normally span the expected life of the project.

NPV will give the best picture of the true value of any investment over a time period [40]. To account for NPV, Malan and Wentzel discount each cost term in the model: e.g., C_{PR}, C_{CR}, C_N, and A. To do this, we apply the following standard net present value equation to each term:

$$Net\ Present\ Value\ =\ \sum_{i=1}^{n} \frac{Cost}{(1\ -\ K)^n}$$

Where:

 $n =$ the number of time periods in the analysis
 $K =$ the discount rate for each time period in the analysis

Malan and Wentzel stress the benefits of accelerated time to market in several ways, giving an enlightening example that most analysts do not consider. Working with forecasts from the marketing department, we can produce an estimate of increased revenue by simply shifting the product's projected revenue stream forward to the product release date that the shortened cycle time from reuse should make possible. One source of additional revenue comes from the interest on the earlier cash flows and profit.

Example: Assume that the sales forecast for new product A comes to 24,000 units at a selling price of $1000. If sales increase by 5000 units at a profit margin of 15%, then profit increases by $750,000 plus interest.

This example illustrates that the profit impact of earlier time to market can significantly affect life-cycle profits.

❖ POULIN AND CARUSO: REUSE METRICS AND ROI

Poulin and Caruso model developed their model at IBM in 1992 in response to the lack of a corporate standard for measuring and reporting software reuse. Despite an extensive software reuse program, IBM had no reliable way to judge the effects or benefits of the investment it had made. Their metrics have the goal of encouraging reuse across IBM, as well as to providing conceptually simple and unobtrusive metrics that realistically reflect the benefits of reuse. The Poulin and Caruso metrics consist of three reuse metrics and two ROI models. The reuse metrics assess reuse levels, the financial benefit of reuse, and the productivity benefit of both reusing and building for reuse. The ROI models provide a tool for simple reuse business case analysis at the project and corporate levels.

REUSE%

The difference between other reuse percent metrics and *Reuse%* comes from the fact that *Reuse%* depends on the definition of reuse, or *RSI*, presented in Chapter 4, "Defining Reuse from a Metrics Point of View." Therefore, if a report appears that gives reuse levels using the symbol *Reuse%*, we can have a high level of confidence in the report and feel comfortable with data supporting the value of *Reuse%*. The metrics also require the total number of source statements in the product. To calculate *Reuse%*, Poulin and Caruso use a standard percent formula:

$$Reuse\% = \frac{RSI}{Total\ Statements} \times 100\%$$

Example: An organization that has developed a 100,000 LOC application determines that 20K LOC of the application meets the definition of *RSI*. The organization calculates the *Reuse%* for the application as:

$$Reuse\% = \frac{RSI}{Total\ Statements} \times 100\%$$

$$= \frac{20,000\ LOC}{100,000\ LOC} \times 100\%$$

$$= 20\%$$

REUSE COST AVOIDANCE

To show the financial benefit of reusing software to an individual project or team, Poulin and Caruso use the *Reuse Cost Avoidance (RCA)* metric. *RCA* represents money an organization did not have to spend to develop new software and therefore estimates the financial benefit of reusing software. *RCA* recognizes cost avoidance takes place:

1. During development
2. During maintenance

While reusing software avoids the cost of developing new software, it still requires effort to locate, assess, and integrate the reused software into your product. Chapter 3, "The Relative Costs of Developing with and for Reuse," showed that the relative cost of reuse (RCR) is only about 20% of the cost of new development. Consequently, we say that the *development cost avoidance (DCA)* corresponds to $(1 - RCR)$ or about 80% of the cost of writing an equivalent amount of custom software. Therefore, development cost avoidance equals:

$$DCA = RSI \times (1 - RCR) \times (New\ code\ cost)$$

$$= RSI \times (1 - 0.2) \times (New\ code\ cost)$$

$$= RSI \times .8 \times (New\ code\ cost)$$

The organization also experiences savings during the maintenance phase of the product. The reusable software suppliers maintain and upgrade the software, so the organization does not have to incur these costs. Although they still have to report problems, reintegrate newer versions of the software, and retest fixes, this cost practically goes to zero when compared to the actual maintenance costs. Therefore, Poulin and Caruso estimate that the *service cost avoidance (SCA)* of the reused software equals 100% of the estimated service cost. They calculate service cost avoidance as:

$$SCA = RSI \times (error\ rate) \times (error\ cost)$$

The final equation for *Reuse Cost Avoidance* equals:

$$RCA = Development\ Cost\ Avoidance + Service\ Cost\ Avoidance$$

"A Reuse Metric Starter Set" on page 97 contains examples of how to apply these metrics.

REUSE VALUE ADDED

The previous two metrics recognize the consumer side of reuse: in other words, the level and the benefit of reusing software. To show how the effectiveness of an organization increases by both reusing software *and* contributing to software reuse, Poulin and Caruso use a reuse leverage metric called the *Reuse Value Added (RVA)*.

The RVA works like a productivity index, where a productivity index equal to 1 indicates normal productivity (productivity equal to one group's work). RVA includes the producer side of reuse by taking into account the software an organization develops for reuse by other organizations. It measures what Poulin and Caruso call *Source Instructions Reused by Others (SIRBO)*.

SIRBO equals the total of all source instructions developed by an organization that other organizations reuse. To calculate SIRBO:

$$SIRBO = \sum (LOC\ per\ part) \times (Organizations\ using\ the\ part)$$

Example: A programming team writes a 10K LOC module in use by five other departments, a 25K LOC macro in use by six other departments, and an unused 75K LOC macro. Then the team has this SIRBO:

$$SIRBO \; = \; (10K\,LOC \; \times \; 5\;depts.) \; + \; (25K\,LOC \; \times \; 6\;depts.)$$

$$+ \; (75K\,LOC \; \times \; 0\;depts.)$$

$$= \; 200K\,LOC$$

An organization's SIRBO increases every time another organization reuses their software. We emphasize a key point: SIRBO only increases if another organization *actually uses* the software. Many metrics and reuse incentive programs fail because they do not make this distinction. If an organization bases a metric or incentive on simply *supplying* "reusable" software, programmers will flood the organization with useless and low-quality routines. SIRBO only measures actual use, so it avoids this problem. To have a high SIRBO a reusable software supplier must do a good job both surveying the need for a component and developing it; consequently, SIRBO makes an excellent metric to use in reuse incentive programs and to assess the true effectiveness of reuse component suppliers [113].

The *Reuse Value Added* metric represents the total effectiveness of a development group resulting from both reusing software and creating software for reuse. We derive the RVA by dividing the total amount of an organization's software in use by the amount of software the organization actually wrote. RVA equals:

$$RVA \; = \; \frac{Total\;Source\;Statements \; + \; SIRBO}{Total\;Source\;Statements \; - \; RSI}$$

Example: Assume a program reused 20K LOC out of a 100K LOC product. In addition, five other departments use a 10K LOC module that the team wrote. The team's RVA equals:

$$RVA \; = \; \frac{100K\,LOC \; + \; (5\;depts. \; \times \; 10K\,LOC)}{100K\,LOC \; - \; 20K\,LOC} \; = \; 1.8$$

The RVA of 1.8 indicates that the team has become 80% more effective through reuse.

Table 17 gives a summary of the three reuse metrics.

TABLE 17	*Poulin and Caruso Reuse Metric Summary*
Metric	*Equation*
Reuse%	$Reuse\% = \dfrac{RSI}{Total\ Source\ Statements} \times 100\%$
Reuse Cost Avoidance (RCA)	*Reuse Cost Avoidance =* *Development Cost Avoidance + Service Cost Avoidance* Where: *Development Cost Avoidance = RSI × (1 − RCR)* *× (New code cost)* *Service Cost Avoidance = RSI × (Error Rate)* *× (Error Cost)*
Reuse Value Added (RVA)	$RVA = \dfrac{Total\ Source\ Statements\ +\ SIRBO}{Total\ Source\ Statements\ -\ RSI}$ Where: $SIRBO = \sum (LOC\ per\ part) \times (Organizations\ using\ the\ part)$

PROJECT-LEVEL ROI

The *Reuse Cost Avoidance* gives the individual team leader or department manager an estimate of the value to that organization of reusing software. However, someone in the organization has to bear the expense of developing and maintaining the software that the individual teams reuse. The manager in charge of the entire development effort needs to account for this by subtracting out these additional costs. Poulin and Caruso call these costs the *Additional Development Cost (ADC)*. They estimate ADC by multiplying the Relative Cost of Writing for Reuse, $RCWR = 1.5$, times the amount of software written for reuse by others. Therefore, ADC equals:

$$ADC = (Relative\ Cost\ of\ Writing\ for\ Reuse\ -\ 1)$$
$$\times (Code\ written\ for\ reuse\ by\ others) \times (New\ code\ cost)$$

Example: To calculate the additional costs to develop 5,000 LOC:

$$ADC = (Relative\ Cost\ of\ Writing\ for\ Reuse\ -\ 1)$$
$$\times (Code\ written\ for\ reuse\ by\ others) \times (New\ code\ cost)$$
$$= (1.5 - 1) \times 5,000\ LOC \times \$100\ per\ line$$
$$= \$250,000$$

Poulin and Caruso call the cost avoidance across a large project the *Project ROI*. When calculating the Project ROI, a manager starts with the sum of the RCAs for all other organizations involved in the project. Poulin and Caruso call this value ORCA, for *Reuse Cost Avoided by Others*:

$$ORCA = \sum RCA_{others}$$

The ROI for the entire project equals the costs avoided by the manager's organization and the costs avoided by other organizations, minus the additional development costs:

$$Project\ ROI = \sum_{i=1}^{n} RCA_i - ADC$$

where i represents the ith organization out of n organizations. "A Reuse Metric Starter Set" on page 97 shows an example use of this metric.

CORPORATE-LEVEL ROI

Unlike projects, which typically run for a limited time, corporate investments include many long-term program costs and have an impact that spans many years. A corporation must make an investment to start a reuse program and then make yearly investments to sustain the program; these investments will generally benefit many projects. For these reasons corporate ROI metrics need to include:

- Costs to start a corporate reuse program
- Reusable Software Library (RSL) costs
- Other reuse tool development and support costs
- Labor and staff for supporting corporate reuse
- License costs for reusable components
- Reuse program costs that spread over multiple projects
- The time value of money

Poulin and Caruso call the corporate investment the *corporate reuse costs*, C. After computing these costs, they discount the corporate ROI using a standard Net Present Value (NPV) analysis. To find the corporate ROI, we start by taking the sum of all Project ROIs for each year of the analysis. This sum equals the revenue savings, R_i, for year i. We then subtract out the corporate reuse costs, C_i, for each year of the analysis. Finally, we apply the NPV equation to discount the reuse investment for each year in the analysis:

$$NPV = C_0 + \frac{R_1}{1+k} + \frac{R_2}{(1+k)^2} + \frac{R_n}{(1+k)^n}$$

Where:

C_O = the corporate reuse start-up costs
R_i = the revenue savings in year i (the sum of all reuse *Project ROIs*)
C_i = corporate reuse costs in year i
n = the time period (years) for the analysis
k = the discount rate

The business decision to invest in reuse depends on the NPV as compared to other investment opportunities. IBM uses NPV in conjunction with decision criteria based on Internal Rate of Return (IRR) to decide on the most favorable investment.

These reuse metrics and ROI models have several key features. First, the definition of reuse clearly identifies what to count. This means that a value for *Reuse%* has a meaning we can trust. The *Reuse Cost Avoided* uses simple, practical, and clear assumptions. This allows managers not only to understand the metric, but also to use it with their own input values to see just how the assumptions affect the manager's bottom line. Finally, the *Reuse Value Added* reflects the overall effect of both reusing and building software for reuse. RVA uses SIRBO because, unlike other metrics, SIRBO only increases with the actual success of the software. Together with the ROI model, these reuse metrics have proven themselves as an effective technology insertion tool.

❖ DEFENSE INFORMATION SYSTEMS AGENCY: REUSE METRICS AND ROI

The United States Defense Information Systems Agency (DISA) uses an extensive set of reuse level and cost avoidance metrics that apply to all U.S. Department of Defense (DoD) contracts [34]. DISA targets specific audiences, e.g., program manager, domain manager, repository manager, program executive, and specifies the metrics to report to each. This section will discuss the DISA metrics for reuse level and cost avoidance. Because DISA based these metrics on the IBM metrics described earlier, they work very much like the Poulin and Caruso model. Most importantly, DISA adopted the definition of RSI, thereby giving the model a counting framework as well as metrics.

Several differences exist between the DISA metrics and the Poulin and Caruso metrics. First, although DISA has metrics for reuse level and cost avoidance, it does not use a productivity index similar to *RVA*. Second, DISA does not include a factor for service cost avoidance. Third, DISA wanted to track the use of modified components in addition to unmodified components. DISA refers to a component used with modifications as *adapted reused code*. DISA separately tracks and reports each of the following code categories:

- Lines of new custom code
- Lines of new reusable code (code written for reuse by others)
- Lines of verbatim reused code (*RSI*)
- Lines of adapted reused code

To report reuse levels, DISA uses a standard reuse percent equation for each category of code, above. For example, a standard reuse report from a program might go as follows: "20% Verbatim Reuse, 30% Adaptive Reuse, 10% New Reusable, and 40% New Custom code." The four values should total 100%.

To determine the impacts of reuse on cost and schedule, the DISA model requires values for the relative costs of reuse for each software category. Based on RCR reports such as those in Chapter 3, the DISA model uses a default value for the relative cost of copying and modifying code of 50%. In other words:

> **White-box reuse costs 50% of the effort of new development.**

The default values for RCR and RCWR remain the same as in the Poulin and Caruso model. DISA recommends using these default values until DISA can compute actual values from completed DISA projects.

The total effort in labor hours to develop a project with reuse, E_R, becomes:

$$E_r = a_1 L_n + a_2 L_r + a_3 L_v + a_4 L_a$$

where:

L_n = lines of new custom code
L_r = lines of new reusable code
L_v = lines of verbatim reused code
L_a = lines of adapted reused code

and the coefficients represent the relative costs of reuse in terms of development hours per line of code as follows:

a_1 = the relative cost of writing custom code (*default* = 1.0)
a_2 = the relative cost of writing reusable code (RCWR) (*default* = 1.5)
a_3 = the relative cost of verbatim reuse (RCR) (*default* = 0.2)
a_4 = the relative cost of adapted reuse (*default* = 0.5)

The DISA cost avoidance equation derives directly from the effort equation. To do this, we multiply each factor by the cost to develop a custom line of code. For U.S. DoD use, DISA suggests a default value of $50 per hour in the model. DISA does not count maintenance costs avoided, but does subtract out the costs of commercial off-the-shelf (COTS) reusable software integrated into the product. Finally, DISA adds a factor to the cost avoidance equation to allow for adaptive reuse.

Example: In a project of 41,000 total LOC, the project reuses 5,000 LOC without modification, reuses another 10,000 LOC with modification, and builds reusable components totalling 1,000 LOC for contribution to the reuse repository. In addition, rather than develop their own abstract data types the project paid $5,000 to purchase a COTS collection of reusable ADTs.

Code Category	Size (LOC)		Effort Coefficient (lines/hour)		Apportioned Effort (hours)
New custom code	25,000	×	1.0	=	25,000
New reusable	1,000	×	1.5	=	1,500
Verbatim reused	5,000	×	0.2	=	1,000
Adapted reused	10,000	×	0.5	=	5,000
Total	41,000 LOC				32,500 hours

Assume a relative cost for the effort in hours per line of new code $a_1 = 1$. To convert the 41,000 LOC needed without reuse (L_n) to units of effort:

$$\text{Effort without reuse equals } E_n = a_1 \times L_n$$

$$= 1.0 \frac{\text{hours}}{\text{LOC}} \times (41,000 \, LOC)$$

$$= 41,000 \text{ hours}$$

So we have the following data:

The estimated effort without reuse $E_n = 41,000 \, hours$
The estimated effort with reuse $E_r = 32,500 \, hours$
The cost of new custom code $R = \$50 \, per \, hour$
$C_{COTS} = \$5000$

This allows us to calculate the cost avoidance for the project:

$$CA_p = R \times (E_n - E_r) - C_{COTS}$$

$$CA_p = \$50/\text{hour} \times (41,000 \text{ hours} - 32,500 \text{ hours}) - \$5000$$

$$CA_p = \$420,000$$

The DISA metrics specify that managers report reuse metrics during project planning and at project completion. The project planning report contributes to the overall project plan and forces the project manager to consider reuse before starting development. The project completion report contains extensive actual data that we can use to adjust the relative cost values during planning for future projects. Furthermore, the data collected can show the actual, as opposed to estimated, benefits of reuse to the project.

❖ CONCLUSION

Each model we have discussed focuses on a particular aspect of reuse in the software development cycle. Having introduced the models in the previous sections, we now summarize the models and their strengths in order to help us choose a model for a particular situation.

REFLECTIONS ON THE MODELS

The Frakes and Terry *reuse level* metrics give both the proportion of a program used repeatedly within a program and the proportion used from sources external to the program, subject to a *threshold level* determined by the user. Because these metrics count *internal reuse*, we have to use caution when choosing these threshold values. Also, their basic metrics for reuse level use *items* as units. This can lead to the problems discussed in question 4 on page 55. To avoid this, Frakes and Terry provide metrics that adjust for the size of components by multiplying each item by the LOC in each item. Because Frakes and Terry provide a tool, *rl*, which implements their metrics, they make a good choice for quickly assessing reuse levels on C programs, subject to the two cautions we have mentioned.

Gaffney and Durek have produced perhaps the best known economic model of reuse. The model inputs the relative costs of reuse (RCR, RCWR), the number of reuses, and reuse level of a program to show the relationship between these values and how they affect total project costs. The model serves as a good theoretical tool for an organization that wants to determine the potential for reuse ROI using its own values for these variables. Because Gaffney and Durek have published the model in several forms, to include a personal-computer-based spreadsheet that implements the model, an organization can easily obtain it and use it in exercises to graphically portray the affects of reuse as shown in Figure 8 on page 69.

Balda and Gustafson extend the popular COCOMO model with terms to allow for a software development cycle with reuse. Their model is intended to help in estimating the total development effort for a project with reuse. The model makes a good choice for organizations just beginning a software development effort and in the process of making resource estimates, especially if the organization already has a familiarity with the COCOMO model. However, the model uses different assumptions regarding the relative costs of reuse (e.g., $RCR = 0.1$ and $RCWR = 2.0$) than are used throughout the rest of this book. Furthermore, an organization *must* calibrate the coefficients in the model before attempting to use it. For this reason we instead recommend using the *Project ROI* equation in "A Reuse Metric Starter Set" on page 97 as an estimating tool.

Barnes and Bollinger provide perhaps the earliest reuse cost–benefit model and apply that model to an organization consisting of many projects. However, as with all C–B models, we must gather and total a significant amount of data for input to the model. This data includes the total estimated costs and benefits of reuse as discussed in "Cost–Benefit Analysis" on page 14. If we have this information, then this model provides a simple and easy decision tool for organizations that want to decide whether or not to invest in a reuse program. However, most organizations do not have this data. This makes it very difficult for a reuse program to apply this or any other C–B model.

Henderson-Sellers uses the same cost–benefit approach to ROI as the Barnes and Bollinger model. Likewise, the Henderson–Sellers model requires us to gather and total all data related to reuse costs and benefits. The model makes a contribution to reuse economics in that it targets the OO audience, but only organizations with access to this C-B data will find it useful. However, with this model we must take care when gathering input data because the reuse counting method used by Henderson-Sellers includes counting software developed for use within an organization and also includes the use of modified software. This will tend to exagerate the benefits due to reuse.

Malan and Wentzel's metrics also use a cost–benefit approach. However, the model differentiates itself from other C-B models by emphasizing the time value of money and the added revenues gained by reduced cycle times. To estimate the number of component reuses, the model uses a probability function instead of actual SIRBO. Like all C-B models, the Malan and Wentzel approach requires us to gather and total a significant amount of data. This makes it difficult to use the model, but it would be a good choice for organizations having this data and also wanting to see the value of reuse over a long period.

The Poulin and Caruso metrics focus on providing realistic estimates of reuse levels and effort saved, based on black-box reuse between organizations. The metrics rely on a consistent counting method for reused software; *RSI* refers to the total absolute measure of reused code that complies with this method. Cost avoidance comes from actual reuses of components rather than estimates; they introduce *Source Instructions*

Reused by Others (SIRBO) to represent the total amount of an organization's software that other organizations have reused. Poulin and Caruso also provide two ROI equations to estimate the total value of reuse to (1) a group of organizations working on a large project (*Project-level ROI*), and, (2) a corporation (*corporate-level ROI*). These metrics make a good choice for organizations able to consistently measure reuse and wanting to see the resulting financial value.

DISA provides a very complete metrics document, including a prescriptive counting model based on the Poulin and Caruso *RSI*. DISA presents reuse-level metrics, cost avoidance metrics, a simple cost–benefit ROI metric, and reuse repository metrics. The DISA metrics document also contains numerous examples and worksheets. Although an organization would not necessarily want to collect all the data and report on all the metrics called out in the document, the DISA reuse metrics document can serve as a good reference for organizations that want to get started in reuse metrics.

TABLE 18 *Summary of Reuse Metric and Economic Models*

Who	Metric	Application

Frakes and Terry	1. Total Reuse Level, based on:
	  a. Internal Reuse Level
	  b. External Reuse Level
	2. Total Reuse Frequency, based on:
	  a. Internal Reuse Frequency
	  b. External Reuse Frequency
		1. To indicate the total proportion of reused code in a program
		2. To indicate the proportion of calls going to functions internal to the program or external to the program

Gaffney and Durek	1. Cost 2. Payoff Threshhold	1. To determine reuse ROI based on the relative costs of reuse (RCR and RCWR), the estimated level of reuse, and the estimated number of reusers 2. To determine the number of reuses necessary for an investment in a reusable component to break even
Balda and Gustafson	LM (reuse estimation model)	To estimate the total effort required to build an application based on COCOMO-based cost drivers and estimates of total application size and amount of reused software

Barnes and Bollinger	1. Q (quality) 2. B (net reuse benefit)	1. Whether or not to make a reuse investment based on the estimated costs and benefits 2. The total financial benefit of reuse across n projects; the number of projects needed to make a reuse investment worthwhile
Henderson-Sellers	1. R (for ROI) 2. R_Q	1. To determine whether to practice reuse on a project based on an estimate of the total costs of reuse activities balanced with the total expected benefits 2. To determine the total ROI (as a ratio) of reuse over Q projects
Malan and Wentzel	S, net cost savings	To determine the financial benefit of reuse as the difference between total costs and benefits, adjusted for fixed costs and the time value of money
Poulin and Caruso	1. Reuse% 2. RCA 3. RVA 4. Project-Level ROI 5. Corporate-Level ROI	1. To accurately reflect and encourage the reuse of unmodified components 2. To provide realistic estimates of the financial benefits of reuse to an organization or application 3. To reflect the combined effect of both reusing and building software for reuse as a productivity index using *SIRBO* 4. To estimate the value of reuse to a group of organizations 5. To estimate the value of reuse across many projects, to include reuse program start-up costs and the time value of money
DISA	1. Reuse Percent 2. Cost avoidance 3. ROI	1. To show code levels by category (new, reusable, reused, modified) 2. To show the financial benefit of reuse to a project 3. To show percent return based on the costs/benefits

❖ 6 ❖

Implementing a Metrics Program

This chapter recommends a highly effective and simple set of reuse metrics. However, to set up a solid metrics program, an organization must have a management structure and process that supports reuse and metrics [144]. This chapter starts by describing the kinds of organizational and process oriented steps that have proven to lead to successful reuse programs. It then prescribes a "Reuse Metrics Starter Set" to use when calculating reuse levels and estimating reuse benefits in any organization.

The management structure described in this chapter dedicates a *Reuse Development Team* to producing and maintaining reusable components for the entire project. This has proved the most effective approach on repeated projects at companies such as IBM, Lockheed Martin Federal Systems [112], and Hewlett-Packard [38, 56]. We show what process activities a typical software development project might adopt in order to incorporate reuse into its processes. The chapter concludes with an extensive case study of a project that uses the organization, processes, and reuse metrics that we describe.

❖ MANAGEMENT STRUCTURE FOR SOFTWARE REUSE

A successful reuse program requires management commitment, emphasis, and continued support. We call the manager's primary contact for reuse on a project the *Reuse Coordinator*. The Reuse Coordinator has overall responsibility for reuse on a project. The Reuse Coordinator works regularly with each organization involved in the project; these organizations assign an individual from their development team the additional responsibility of *Reuse Lead* for that organization. The organization Reuse Leads help their respective organizations by hunting for reuse opportunities and, working with the Project Reuse Coordinator, by identifying components for use by other organizations. Together, the Reuse Coordinator and all the organization Reuse Leads form a *Reuse Working Group* for the project. This section will discuss in detail the responsibilities of each of these people and groups.

SOFTWARE DEVELOPMENT MANAGER FOR THE PROJECT

The Chief Software Development Manager on a project has sole responsibility for maintaining emphasis on reuse and providing the resources to ensure that reuse succeeds. The manager will:

1. Designate one technical person to serve as the full-time project Reuse Coordinator and ensure that each organization has assigned a part-time organization Reuse Lead.

2. Allocate time to the project Reuse Coordinator to educate and train each member of the development staff as necessary.

3. Allocate resources to the Librarian/Reuse Development Team for the identification, development, and maintenance of reusable components (software developed during a project to provide common services to the project).

4. Establish reuse level baselines and set reuse goals for each organization.

5. *Regularly request and track software reuse metrics.*

PROJECT REUSE COORDINATOR

The project Reuse Coordinator has primary responsibility for the implementation of a reuse program and serves as the focal point for sharing information among all organizations on a project. In this role, this full-time person must be generally familiar with all available software and must constantly process who-does-what and who-needs-what. The Reuse Coordinator:

1. Leads the project reuse effort.

2. Identifies opportunities for interproject reuse.

3. Searches reuse libraries, the Internet, and the World Wide Web (WWW) for components that might meet project requirements.

4. Plans for and coordinates reuse education and training.

5. Works with the organization Reuse Leads to evaluate and share reuse experiences from each organization.

6. Publicizes available shareable resources as appropriate.

7. Ensures easy access to shareable resources.

8. Ensures that shareable resources comply with the project configuration management policy so that all projects using a component receive notification of any changes made to the component.

9. Works with software management and project management on all project reuse issues.

10. Ensures that all shared components have no legal restrictions on their use.

11. Participates in application requirements reviews, design reviews, and inspections to help identify reusable components. Provides management with technical evaluations of reuse versus new development trade-offs.

12. Assists management in coordinating the development of interproject reusable components.

13. Leads the Reuse Working Group.

14. *Captures and analyzes reuse metrics and provides regular status reports to management.*

Having a good Reuse Coordinator usually results in having a successful reuse program. Having a weak Reuse Coordinator will almost certainly have the opposite result. Therefore, we look for Reuse Coordinators who have a genuine commitment to reuse and who act with enthusiasm and discretion.

ORGANIZATION REUSE LEADS

The responsibility for reuse within an organization falls on the part-time organization "Reuse Lead." This person works with the project Reuse Coordinator to find needed components and helps other organization Reuse Leads locate components for their organizations. Because the Reuse Lead has responsibility for all reuse activities within the organization, the Reuse Lead will perform many of the same actions as the Reuse Coordinator, but on a more limited scale. The job includes reporting reuse activities to the Reuse Coordinator, especially the names and sizes of components that the organization reuses. The Reuse Coordinator needs this input to calculate the project reuse metrics. Finally, the Reuse Lead serves as a member of the Reuse Working Group.

REUSE WORKING GROUP

All the Reuse Leads form the Reuse Working Group for the project. The Reuse Coordinator chairs the Reuse Working Group on behalf of the Software Development Manager. The group promotes software reuse: it identifies, reviews, and approves reuse components, it tracks reuse metrics, and it coordinates and controls reuse development. The group meets once per week or as needed to provide a forum to identify reuse components and to discuss issues related to existing components.

REUSE DEVELOPMENT TEAM AND LIBRARIAN

Responsibility for the final design, development, support, and configuration control of reusable components lies with the Reuse Development Team. As a support organization, this team reports directly to the Reuse Development Manager and falls under the technical operational control of the Reuse Coordinator.

Figure 9 depicts a typical organization for a large software development project. As shown in the figure, this team enjoys a status equal to the other organizations working on the project. The team assesses change requests, prioritizes requests for new components, and controls modifications to existing components. As the project and collection of shared resources grows, one member of the team may have to devote full time to administrative functions related to the components, especially configuration control. We call this person the Reuse Librarian.

APPLICATION DEVELOPERS

All members of the project must remain aware of components available for reuse and incorporate those components into their work products. Developers also help identify modules and other work products that might find use in other organizations and bring them to the attention of their Reuse Lead. Every person has a role and participates in the development and implementation of a successful software reuse program.

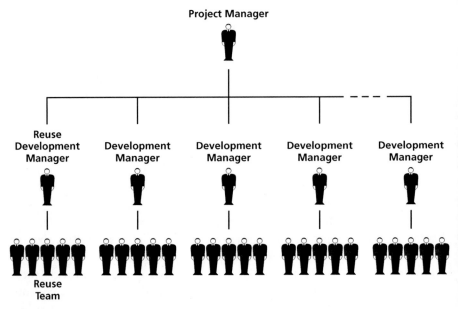

FIGURE 9 *Management Structure for Reuse on a Large Project*

❖ THE SOFTWARE DEVELOPMENT PROCESS WITH REUSE

As development organizations move through the development cycle, they take every opportunity to examine where they can save effort through the reuse of existing resources. This applies as much to information such as designs and test cases as it does to source code. As the organizations iterate through the development cycle, the Reuse Leads examine available resources and try to locate existing work products rather than redevelop them.

Other than emphasizing the use of existing components throughout the life cycle, the basic software development process for an organization remains unchanged. The organizations define requirements and perform design activities in accordance with sound software engineering principles [114]. However, in development with reuse, significant savings may come from tailoring requirements, designs, and other application work products early in the development cycle based on knowledge of existing reusable components.

In other words, designers and developers should actively work to modify the application in order to reuse previous work. This may mean making a business decision as to whether to possibly postpone, drop, or change the details of a specific requirement. Benefits to the organization include allowing application programmers to develop within a consistent framework and to make maximum use of resources. Benefits to the customer include ensuring a consistent look, feel, and behavior of applications while reducing the overall cost.

Table 19 depicts reuse-related milestones that occur during software development. Although the table uses terms normally associated with a waterfall model, the milestones apply equally well in any process model. For example, if an organization follows a spiral or incremental approach, the organization can apply the milestone at each iteration of development.

TABLE 19 *Reuse Milestones in Software Development*

Phase	*Task (1)*

Planning and Business Engineering Phase	◆ Designate Project Reuse Coordinator (RC)
	◆ Designate Organization Reuse Leads (RLs)
	◆ RLs contact RC
	◆ RC identifies RLs and forms the Reuse Working Group (RWG)
	    ◆ RLs read and understand reuse policies
	    ◆ Hold kick-off RWG meeting

	◆ Establish file structure and management plan for configuration management
	◆ Define/grant directory and file system access modes
	◆ Conduct preliminary reuse opportunity assessment based on search of available component collections
	◆ RLs meet with RC to define search parameters and search external sources (e.g., WWW) and reuse libraries
	◆ Obtain identified software and place in directories
	◆ Conduct initial market survey of applicable COTS products
	◆ Prepare hard/soft catalog of available components
	◆ Set project reuse goals
	◆ Establish baseline from previous projects
	◆ Set aggressive and realistic goals
System Review	◆ Present findings, rationale, and reuse goals
Requirements Analysis Phase	◆ Review reuse opportunities by examining organizations with related requirements
	◆ Meet with other RLs
	◆ Propose common functions to RC for development by the Reuse Development Team
	◆ Examine components previously built by the Reuse Development Team
	◆ Identify and select reusable work products
	◆ Identify candidate COTS software components from market analysis
	◆ Make list of candidate COTS software
	◆ Prepare reuse metric collection plan with RC
	◆ Understand required data and tool support
	◆ Understand metrics and reporting frequency
Requirements Review	◆ Present findings and rationale from Requirements Analysis Phase
High-Level Design Phase	◆ Review for detailed design reuse candidates and potential for function common with other organizations
	◆ Evaluate and select, through a formal trade study, reusable COTS software components from the list of candidates
	◆ Document COTS decisions on selected/rejected components
	◆ Make estimate of final reuse level and commit to the application reuse goal

High-Level Design Review	◆ Present findings and rationale from the High-Level Design Phase
Design and Development Phase	◆ Coordinate all reuse activity
	◆ Hold weekly Reuse Working Group meetings
	◆ Review for code reuse candidates within each organization
	◆ Analyze and select components for reuse across organizations
	◆ Document rationale for selected/rejected components
	◆ Integrate selected components into application
	◆ Ensure that new development adheres to sound software engineering principles and characteristics of reusable software
	◆ Collect and prepare initial software metric data
	◆ Update application reuse estimate
	◆ Compare final reuse level to goal
	◆ Review test case reuse candidates
Integration and Test Phase	◆ Select test case candidates
	◆ Complete collection of software development data and calculate reuse metrics
	◆ Integrate and test reused components with other software
Deployment Phase	◆ Measure performance against reuse goals
	◆ Assess reuse metrics and impact

NOTE: Each task takes place on every iteration.

❖ A REUSE METRIC STARTER SET

We recommend the following metrics as a starting point for any organization. They make a simple, easy-to-understand set that can quickly convey the amount of software reused and the benefits that reuse brings to an organization or project:

1. *Reuse%* for measuring reuse levels

2. *Reuse Cost Avoidance* (*RCA*) for quantifying the benefits of reusing software to an organization

3. *Project ROI* for estimating reuse benefits across multiple organizations

RECOMMENDED METRIC: MEASURING THE LEVEL OF REUSE

Use the de facto industry standard with the added strength of RSI to give credibility to the value. Report reuse levels using *Reuse%* as follows:

$$Reuse\% \ = \ \frac{RSI}{Total\ Statements} \ \times \ 100\%$$

Example: If your programming team developed and maintains 90K LOC and also uses 10K LOC from an external source, your team's *Reuse%* equals:

$$Reuse\% \ = \ \frac{10K\ LOC}{10K\ LOC \ + \ 90K\ LOC} \ \times \ 100\% \ = \ 10\%$$

RECOMMENDED METRIC: MEASURING THE BENEFITS OF REUSE TO AN ORGANIZATION

For starters, use the simple formula for *Reuse Cost Avoidance (RCA)*. For the relative costs of reuse, you can use the default values of $RCR = 0.2$ and $RCWR = 1.5$, unless you have data that you feel better represents your organization's actual values. To calculate Reuse Cost Avoidance:

$$RCA \ = \ Development\ Cost\ Avoidance \ + \ Service\ Cost\ Avoidance$$

Where *Development Cost Avoidance (DCA):*

$$DCA \ = \ RSI \ \times \ (1 \ - \ RCR) \ \times \ (New\ code\ cost)$$

And *Service Cost Avoidance (SCA):*

$$SCA \ = \ RSI \ \times \ (Your\ error\ rate) \ \times \ (Your\ error\ cost)$$

Example: If your development cost for new code equals $100 per line, then your DCA for 20K LOC RSI equals:

$$DCA \ = \ RSI \ \times \ (1 \ - \ RCR) \ \times \ (New\ code\ cost)$$

$$= \ 20K\ LOC \ \times \ (1 \ - \ RCR) \ \times \ \$100\ per\ line$$

$$= \ 20K\ LOC \ \times \ (1 \ - \ 0.2) \ \times \ \$100\ per\ line$$

$$= \ 20K\ LOC \ \times \ .8 \ \times \ \$100\ per\ line$$

$$= \ \$1.6\ million$$

If your error rate for new code equals 1.5 errors per thousand LOC, and if your cost to fix an error equals $10K, then your *SCA* for 20K LOC RSI equals:

$$SCA = RSI \times (Your\ Error\ Rate) \times (Your\ Error\ Cost)$$

$$= 20K\ LOC \times 1.5\ errors\ per\ K\ LOC \times \$10K\ per\ error$$

$$= \$0.3\ million$$

Putting it all together, your *RCA* equals:

$$RCA = Development\ Cost\ Avoidance + Service\ Cost\ Avoidance$$

$$= \$1.6\ million + \$0.3\ million$$

$$= \$1.9\ million$$

To account for writing reusable components . . .

The basic *RCA* metric assumes your organization only consumes reusable software. If you also produce reusable software, you can simply subtract your *Additional Development Cost (ADC)* from your organization's *RCA* to obtain your organization's *ROI*:

$$ADC = (RCWR - 1) \times (Code\ written\ for\ reuse\ by\ others) \times (New\ code\ cost)$$

Example: If your programming team developed 3K LOC for reuse by other organizations, you incurred:

$$ADC = (RCWR - 1) \times (Code\ written\ for\ reuse\ by\ others) \times (New\ code\ cost)$$

$$= (1.5 - 1) \times 3K\ LOC \times (\$100\ per\ line)$$

$$= \$0.15\ million$$

To continue our example, this means your organization has an organizational ROI_{org}:

$$ROI_{org} = RCA - ADC$$

$$ROI_{org} = \$1.9\ million - \$0.15\ million$$

$$= \$1.75\ million$$

RECOMMENDED METRIC: MEASURING REUSE BENEFITS ACROSS A PROJECT

If all the organizations working on a project have calculated their RCA values and adjusted the value for additional development costs to find their organizational ROIs, the project manager can simply total these values to find the ROI for the project:

$$Project\ ROI\ =\ \sum ROI_{org}$$

Note that the project manager can achieve the same result by taking the sum of the unadjusted RCAs and then subtract off the ADC for the entire project. The equation to do this appears as the *Project ROI* equation in "Project-Level *ROI*" on page 81:

$$Project\ ROI\ =\ \sum_{i=1}^{n} RCA_i\ -\ ADC$$

where *i* represents the *i*th organization out of *n* organizations. The following case study shows how to use these metrics.

❖ CASE STUDY: APPLYING REUSE METRICS ON A PROJECT

Lockheed Martin Federal Systems (LMFS) develops a large distributed, interactive training system for the U.S. Army called the Close Combat Tactical Trainer (CCTT) [90]. CCTT allows soldiers to fight simulated combat scenarios in a high-fidelity re-creation of mechanized vehicle equipment and terrain. As part of the system, LMFS had to develop software to simulate the mobility and firepower of various vehicles on the simulated battlefield. The project employs approximately 300 engineers and has developed over 1.2 million lines of Ada software. LMFS delivered six iterations, or *builds*, of the CCTT software over a two-year period.

CCTT currently has 16 *application areas*, which correspond to the simulation software for each of the vehicles. The vehicles include the M1A1 Tank, M1A2 Tank, M113 Personnel Carrier, and the M2A2 Bradley Fighting Vehicle. Because of the high potential to reuse software for each of these vehicles, LMFS planned for reuse, organized for reuse, and collected reuse metrics from the beginning of the project.

For the purposes of reuse metrics, CCTT uses the definition of RSI defined in Chapter 4, "Defining Reuse from a Metrics Point of View." Specifically, software used without modification by more than one application area counts as reuse. Note that the size of these application areas ranges from approximately 20K LOC up to about 180K LOC. CCTT also has defined application areas for shared *system services*. When a vehicle simulation application area uses this software, it counts as reuse.

CCTT built most of their own reusable components for use across application areas. They also obtained some reusable components from reuse libraries managed by organizations external to the project. Because CCTT wanted to track the level of reuse from the domain-specific components they built separately from those that they obtained externally, CCTT reports these reuse levels as *domain-specific reuse* and *external reuse*. This distinction just adds one piece of information to the recommended metrics.

To gather the data required for reuse metrics, the CCTT Reuse Coordinator starts by running a commercial code metrics tool on the CCTT source files. The tool allows the Reuse Coordinator to find the size of each component in CCTT and generates a listing of each component used within an application area. She then sorts the components by source. Figure 10 gives an extract of the more than 200 pages of output listings produced when calculating the reuse metrics for Build 6 of CCTT.

Combining the size of each component with the listing of components used by each application allows the Reuse Coordinator to calculate RSI for each application area. Table 20 shows the reuse metrics worksheet for CCTT. This worksheet looks very much like the worksheets in "Appendix A: Reuse Metric Worksheets" on page 153, with the addition of a column to distinguish between reuse from domain-specific and that from externally obtained reuse components.

Domain-specific reusable components used by the AAR application area:

```
/cctt/common/environment/build6/dynamic_terrain
/cctt/common/environment/build6/environment_entity
/cctt/common/environment/build6/terrain_database
   . . .
```

Externally obtained reusable components used by the AAR application area:

```
/cctt/system_services/container_classes/lists
/cctt/system_services/container_classes/maps
/cctt/system_services/container_classes/queues
/cctt/system_services/container_classes/semaphores
/cctt/system_services/container_classes/stacks
/cctt/system_services/container_classes/storage_managers
/cctt/system_services/container_classes/utilities
/cctt/system_services/os_interfaces/posix
   . . .
```

FIGURE 10 *Extract of Components Used by a CCTT Application, by Source*

| **TABLE 20** | *CCTT RSI by Application Area for Build 6* |

Application Area	RSI from external sources	Domain-specific RSI	LOC written for reuse	New or changed LOC	Total LOC
AAR	8,338	38,032	5,619	24,038	76,027
EM	4,452	6,427	0	2,535	13,414
MCC/MC	7,346	29,892	1,694	28,398	67,330
System Services	1,119	0	11,196	10,119	22,434
PVD	6,429	7,309	336	26,835	40,909
M1A1	11,132	23,452	79,385	62,765	176,734
M1A2	11,828	102,393	0	19,397	133,618
M113A3	10,941	93,448	0	4,479	108,868
M2M3	10,941	88,964	0	8,600	108,505
UOSP	0	0	0	23,849	23,849
CGF	6,500	11,011	120,663	0	138,174
SAF	7,248	51,991	2,346	40,178	101,763
DI	8,741	138,478	0	15,069	162,288
OC WS	8,022	49,819	3,084	37,135	98,060
Protocol Translator	0	0	0	1,500	1,500
Trainer Support	0	0	0	22,685	22,685
Totals:	103,037	641,216	224,323	327,582	1,296,158

The RSI for CCTT comes from both the reusable components obtained from external sources and the domain-specific components. Therefore:

$$RSI \ = \ 103,037 \ LOC \ + \ 641,216 \ LOC \ = \ 744,253 \ LOC$$

We can now easily calculate the Reuse% for CCTT using the formula:

$$Reuse\% \ = \ \frac{RSI}{Total \ Statements} \times 100\%$$

$$= \ \frac{744,253 \ LOC}{1,296,158 \ LOC} \times 100\%$$

$$= \ 57.4\%$$

Table 21 details the resulting reuse levels by showing the values of *Reuse%* for each application area. The numbers in the table contain several lessons for domain-specific reuse. Note that the application area that provides common code for the vehicle simulation application areas (i.e., system services) has little or no reuse. Also

TABLE 21 *CCTT Reuse% by Application Area for Build 6*

Application Area	Total LOC per application area	Percent of domain-specific reuse	Percent of external reuse	Total Reuse%
AAR	76,027	50.0%	11.0%	61.0%
EM	13,414	47.9%	33.2%	81.1%
MCC/MC	67,330	44.4%	10.9%	55.3%
System Services	22,434	0%	5.0%	5.0%
PVD	40,909	17.9%	15.7%	33.6%
M1A1	176,734	13.3%	6.3%	19.6%
M1A2	133,618	76.6%	8.9%	85.5%
M113A3	108,868	85.8%	10.0%	95.9%
M2M3	108,505	82.0%	10.1%	92.1%
UOSP	23,849	0%	0%	0%
CGF	138,174	8.0%	4.7%	12.7%
SAF	101,763	51.1%	7.1%	58.2%
DI	162,288	85.3%	5.4%	90.7%
OC WS	98,060	50.8%	8.2%	59.0%
Protocol Translator	1,500	0%	0%	0%
Trainer Support	22,685	0%	0%	0%
Totals:	**1,296,158**	**49.5%**	**7.9%**	**57.4%**

note that the M1A1 Tank simulation had a relatively low *Reuse%*, 19.6%. However, the subsequent simulation for the M1A2 Tank had a much higher *Reuse%*, 85.5%, indicating how well CCTT engineered their domain-specific software for use on multiple applications.

Although we do not have actual ROI numbers from CCTT, we can take the LOC numbers in the report to estimate the benefits of reuse to CCTT as compared to CCTT having to write each vehicle simulation without any reuse. We do this with the *Project ROI* calculations. Since we have already summed the LOC to find the totals for CCTT, we only need to calculate the CCTT RCA using these totals and subtract out the Additional Development Costs (ADC). We will use default values for all of our input metrics and assume that they apply to every organization:

$RCR = 0.2$
$RCWR = 1.5$
New code cost = \$100/LOC
Error rate = 1 error/KLOC
Error cost = \$10K/error

First, we calculate the RCA by estimating the costs avoided during development and the costs avoided during maintenance:

$$DCA = RSI \times (1 - RCR) \times New\ code\ cost$$

$$= 744{,}253\ LOC \times (1 - 0.2) \times \$100\ per\ line$$

$$= 744{,}253\ LOC \times .8 \times \$100\ per\ line$$

$$= \$59{,}540{,}240$$

$$SCA = RSI \times Error\ rate \times Error\ cost$$

$$= 744{,}253\ LOC \times 1\ errors\ per\ KLOC \times \$10K\ per\ error$$

$$= \$7{,}442{,}530$$

This allows us to calculate the CCTT RCA:

$$RCA = Development\ Cost\ Avoidance + Service\ Cost\ Avoidance$$

$$= \$59{,}540{,}240 + \$7{,}442{,}530$$

$$= \$66{,}982{,}770$$

Next, we calculate the ADC we estimate that CCTT incurred to develop the domain-specific reusable components:

$$ADC = (RCWR - 1) \times (Code\ written\ for\ reuse\ by\ others) \times (New\ code\ cost)$$

$$= (1.5 - 1) \times 224{,}323\ LOC \times \$100\ per\ line$$

$$= \$11{,}216{,}150$$

Therefore, the ROI for the entire CCTT project equals:

$$Project\ ROI = \sum_{i=1}^{n} RCA_i - ADC$$

$$= Project\ RCA - ADC$$

$$= \$66{,}982{,}770 - \$11{,}216{,}150$$

$$= \$55{,}766{,}620$$

The *Project ROI* = \$55,766,620 estimates the cost avoided compared to doing the entire CCTT project by writing each vehicle simulation application with nothing but custom software. While we do not have actual budget data from CCTT, we can use these experiences when planning for upcoming projects. The impressive results can help justify investments that lead to a similar reuse strategy of organizing for reuse and investing in reusable components for use across a large project.

We conclude the case study by showing the long-term effects of domain-specific reuse on CCTT. The CCTT Reuse Coordinator tracks reuse metrics over time by recording the levels for each build. Figure 11 illustrates how the CCTT *Reuse%* has increased with each system build. As with the previous tables, the graph breaks down the overall *Reuse%* by the levels of reuse coming from external sources and from domain-specific components.

As expected for the first build, CCTT received all reuse from external sources because CCTT had not yet developed its domain-specific components. However, the level of domain-specific reuse steadily grows with each build to quickly become the driving factor in CCTT reuse. The graph shows that the contribution of external components quickly peaks at around 15%.[11] This situation mirrors the discussion presented in "Expected Levels of Reuse" on page 5. CCTT serves as a classic example of successful domain-specific reuse, and of how to apply reuse metrics on a large project.

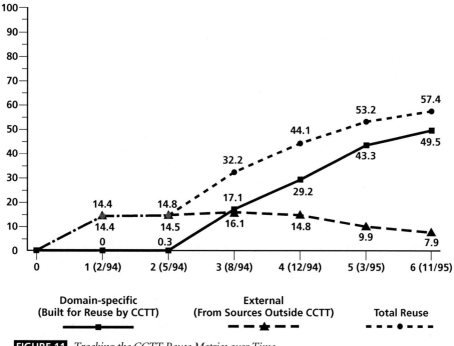

FIGURE 11 *Tracking the CCTT Reuse Metrics over Time*

---

[11] The percent decline starting with build number 4 is due to the increase in size of CCTT; in absolute terms, CCTT uses about the same KLOC of externally obtained software in every build.

❖ MAINTAINING A REUSE METRICS PROGRAM

One final caution for organizations dealing with reuse metrics: Having even a well-defined metric model does not mean that we have solved the reuse counting and reporting problem. Organizations will continue to try to make numbers say what they want them to say. Keeping reuse reports accurate and equitable requires diligence.

Sometimes the organization simply ignores instructions on reporting software metrics. In one example, an Army program manager ordered a contractor to count COTS products as reuse so the program manager would "look better" in his progress reports. We must often explain the rationale for our metric models; ensuring accurate reports requires constant oversight!

In another case, two years after these metrics went into effect in IBM, an executive asked for a review of how different sites had done with regard to reuse levels. Having worked with the sites for some time, we knew which had strong and aggressive reuse programs, and which did not. Consequently, one site, which develops a major embedded control systems product, stood out as having an unexpectedly high level of reported reuse. Either they had made a major turnaround in their program that would make a nice showcase for others, or they had a problem with their metrics calculation. We contacted the person responsible for metrics at that site. It did not take long to see that a calculation problem caused the unexpectedly high numbers. They counted *base code* in their metrics for every new version of the product. We asked the site metrics coordinator:

> "Why do you include *base code* in all your metrics?"
> "We always have, for as long as I remember," he replied.
> "Don't you know that doesn't follow the corporate measurement guidelines?"
> "Yes. . . ."
> "Don't you know that doesn't follow your *division's measurement* guidelines?"
> "Yes. . . ."

Whereupon the metrics coordinator explained that the corporate and division guidelines really did not matter to the local management and they would report metrics the way they wanted to report them (this discovery revealed a much larger management problem).

A third case involved a site which had reported a good level of reuse, but not one that seemed unreasonably high given the strength of their program. Something on the report attracted our attention, however. Most of their reuse came from a couple of small projects, whereas the major programs seemed largely to ignore any systematic reuse activity. It turned out that they had *averaged the reuse percents of all projects* to arrive at the reuse percent for the site. This, we pointed out, simply did not follow the rules of mathematics. You can't average percents.

❖ CONCLUSION

This chapter starts with an example management structure and process for implementing a reuse program. The management structure centers on a *Reuse Coordinator*, who has responsibility for leading all reuse activities on a project. The structure also calls for a *Reuse Development Team*, which has responsibility for building and maintaining the shared software on a project. However, these special roles receive help from reuse representatives throughout the project, from organization *Reuse Leads* to individual developers. Of course, the entire reuse program depends on dedicated managers to commit the will and resources needed to fully integrate reuse into the software development cycle and make reuse "Business as Usual" for the organization.

The chapter then prescribes a recommended "Reuse Metrics Starter Set" for organizations:

- *Reuse%* for measuring reuse levels,
- *Reuse Cost Avoidance* for estimating the costs avoided by reusing software in an organization or application, and
- *Project ROI*, for estimating the benefits of reusing and producing software for reuse across multiple organizations.

These metrics can provide all the information most organizations need to report their reuse activity. To illustrate the use of the metrics, this chapter presented a case study of a large project that has successfully implemented a reuse program and reports their progress using these metrics.

❖ 7 ❖

Measuring
Software Reusability

This chapter examines various approaches to measuring software reusability. Knowing what makes software "reusable" can teach us how to build new reusable components and help us to identify potentially useful modules in legacy software. This chapter begins by establishing a taxonomy of approaches to reusability metrics based on their empirical or qualitative orientation. It then examines the disciplines, theories, and techniques used by numerous existing reusability measurement methods as they relate to the taxonomy. Recognizing that most of these methods focus exclusively on internal characteristics of components and ignore environmental factors, this chapter challenges reusability researchers to incorporate software architecture and domain attributes into their metrics. We will see that the application domain and software architecture are critical factors in component reusability. The research, framework, and conclusions in this chapter provide a useful reference for persons interested in ways to determine the reusability of software [110].

❖ MOTIVATION

Many software engineers believe software reuse provides the key to enormous savings and benefits in software development; the U.S. Department of Defense alone could save $300 million annually by increasing its level of reuse by as little as 1% [2]. However, we have yet to identify a reliable way to quantify what we mean by "reusable" software. Such a measure may not only help us learn how to build reusable components, but also help us identify reusable components among the wealth of existing programs.

Existing programs contain years of knowledge and experience gained from working in an application domain and meeting an organization's software needs. If we could extract this information efficiently, we could gain a valuable resource upon which to build future applications. Unfortunately, working with existing software poses several significant problems due to inconsistent quality, style, documentation, and design across legacy systems.

This chapter examines metrics used to determine the *reusability* of software components. In light of the recent emphasis on software reuse, numerous research efforts have attempted to quantify our ability to use a component in new contexts. This research has identified many objective and subjective criteria that contribute to the question:

> **What makes software reusable?**

One possible measure of a component's reusability comes from its *successful use*: how many times do other applications access this common code? Other measures come from *static code metrics* generated automatically by a variety of commercial tools. Many of the known empirical methods use a version of complexity metrics to measure reusability. We can also devise *qualitative measures* of reusability: adherence to formatting standards and style guidelines, completeness of testing, and existence of supporting information such as integration instructions and design documentation. This chapter examines these various approaches to measuring software reusability.

❖ A TAXONOMY OF REUSABILITY METRICS

Approaches to measuring reusability fall into two basic methods: *empirical* and *qualitative*. Empirical methods have a very desirable characteristic: they depend on objective data, and a tool or analyst can usually calculate them automatically and cheaply. The qualitative methods generally rely on a subjective assessment of the software's adherence to some guidelines or principles. Although this allows us to attach a value to an abstract concept, collecting qualitative data often requires substantial manual effort and personal judgment. This tends to make qualitative methods more expensive and more error-prone than empirical methods.

Within each method, the metrics tend to focus in one of two areas. In the first, the metrics address attributes unique to the code itself, such as the number of source statements it contains, its complexity, or the tests it successfully passed. We call these methods *module-oriented*. In the second approach, the metrics take into account other reusable assets related to the module, such as the presence and/or quality of supporting documentation. When we refer to a method that considers the module and all of these supporting pieces of information, we call it *component-oriented*. This book will present software reusability methods using the taxonomy in Figure 12.

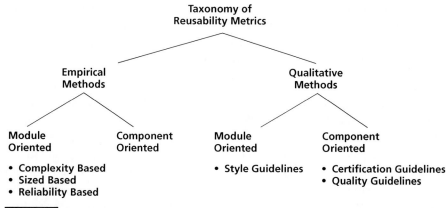

FIGURE 12 *Taxonomy of Reusability Metrics*

RELATED WORK

We can relate reusability to *portability*, since both involve the use of a component in a new context [102]. A 1990 U.S. Department of Defense report concluded that the ultimate measure of portability comes from the number of source lines of code that a programmer needs to change to get a module to execute in a different environment. This study recommended developing a mathematical function to convert the amount of changed code to a portability value. However, the study went on to state that it could not base any conclusions on reusability factors.

Software *complexity* metrics reveal internal characteristics of a module, collection of modules, or object-oriented programs [28]. Studies indicate that complex modules cost the most to develop and have the highest rates of failure. It follows that we will find modules with desirable complexity values more reusable than modules with undesirable values. McCabe and Halstead developed the two most widely known complexity metrics:

- The McCabe Cyclomatic Complexity metric links the number of logical branches (decisions) in a module to the difficulty of programming [94]. McCabe melds a graph theory approach with software engineering: if you represent the logic structure of a module using a flowchart (a graph) and count the regions of the graph caused by program flow statements (*do–while, if–then–else*), the number of regions in the graph corresponds to the complexity of the program. If the number of regions, $V(G)$, exceeds 10, the module may have too many changes of control.

- Halstead's Software Science metrics link studies on human cognitive ability to software complexity [57]. Halstead's approach parses the program or problem statement into tokens and classifies the tokens into operators (verbs, functions, procedures) and operands (nouns, variables, files). Equations based on these tokens give program complexity in terms of a variety of indicators, including estimated effort, program volume, and size.

Not surprisingly, basic software engineering principles address many of the aspects of software that might make software reusable. This particularly applies to those qualities that make software *maintainable*. One study based on this premise constructs a taxonomy of 92 attributes affecting the ease of maintaining software [149]. Among other findings, the study concludes that maintenance effort correlates highly with the Halstead complexity metrics, a finding almost universally corroborated by reusability researchers. However, at least one researcher came to exactly the opposite conclusion, finding that maintenance effort (as measured by fault distribution) does *not* correlate with the Halstead metrics [95].

Program comprehension relates closely to program complexity, because perceived complexity affects how well a user can comprehend the program [150]. Criteria and conditions for program comprehension show that we can translate theoretical numerical measures from software complexity back to empirical conditions. This means that we can describe program comprehension with empirical axioms. From the software reuse perspective, we could use these techniques to identify potentially reusable components. For example, Canfora *et al.* built a prototype tool that uses candidate criteria to identify abstract data types in existing program code [24]. The tool applies the criteria in an experiment that analyzes five different programs (1) for the purpose of reverse engineering/reengineering and (2) to identify and extract reusable components from the programs.

Another factor affecting whether a programmer will choose to use an existing component in a new situation is how quickly the programmer can assimilate what the component does and how to use it. *Program understanding* methods address this problem. These methods attempt to present the important information about a component to the user in a way the user can quickly assess [96]. For example, recognizing that expert programmers organize the important information about a component into mental templates, Linn and Clancy developed a visual template containing this same information. Their study shows that using a standard layout lets a potential reuser quickly scan the important aspects of a component, such as text descriptions, pseudo-code, illustrations, and implementation information [86]. Understanding how good reusable software works not only helps the programmer learn how to write good reusable software; it increases the chances the programmer will use more of what already exists.

The discussion of what makes software reusable has taken place for a long time. In 1984 Matsumoto stressed qualities such as these:

1. Generality,
2. Definiteness (the degree of clarity or understandability),
3. Transferability (portability), and
4. Retrievability

as the major characteristics leading to the reusability of a component [92]. However, empirical measures remain elusive. We will now discuss some of the reasons for this.

ISSUES SURROUNDING REUSABILITY MEASUREMENT

One reason why we find it so hard to develop reusability metrics comes from the fact that no one completely understands "design for reuse" issues [16]. Given that we often do not agree on what makes a component reusable, obtaining an equation that quantifies the concept offers a significant challenge. To put it simply, we need to define reusability before we can quantify it.

To illustrate this point, Woodfield, Embley, and Scott conducted an experiment where 51 developers had to assess the reusability of an Abstract Data Type (ADT) in 21 different situations [147]. They found developers untrained in reuse did poorly; the developers based their decisions on unimportant factors such as size of the ADT and ignored other important factors. As a result, the study recommends developing tools and education that can help developers assess components for reuse.

Once we identify a potentially reliable metric, we need to look at something we call *causality*. Reusability metrics must carefully separate the factors contributing to reusability. In other words, if we find that smaller modules get reused more often, does this mean the small size made the module more reusable, and therefore we should build all reusable modules small? Wouldn't we receive greater benefits from reusing larger components? In a detailed examination of module size on reusability, Esteva sought to develop an automated tool for identifying reusable components in C and C++ programs [37]. The research focused on trying to characterize the kinds of knowledge that developers typically use while searching for reusable components. Using the hypothesis that developers will tend to reuse components that they comprehend most easily, the researchers tested to see if small, simple, well-documented components correlate highly with what expert programmers consider "reusable." Using standard size and complexity metrics such as lines of code, the researchers found that the tool agreed 80% of the time (12 out of 15 examples) with the aggregate reusability score given by expert software engineers. This finding may lead us to believe that reusability lies exclusively in the realm of those components consisting of relatively few lines of code.

Unlike reuse-level metrics, which derive from directly observable measures of software size, reusability metrics often combine many attributes to obtain a general reusability value. This introduces a number of issues related to metric theory. For example, if a reusability metric involves a wide variety of input parameters, we must examine the interrelationships among the parameters and their relative importance. We look for certain qualities such as statistical independence [41]; well-formed metrics should not have any correlations among the elements that make up the metric [77]. Although these issues primarily concern metric theorists, the practitioner can also benefit. For example, if "lines of code" truly indicate "reusability" as discussed earlier, then we do not need to develop expensive methods and tools to identify reusable modules.

Finally, some metric values may give conflicting reuse information. For example, do we desire a low value or a high value for a given attribute? Consider module "complexity." Complex modules may indicate potential trouble spots and warrant additional testing, redesign, or further decomposition. However, some algorithms may have high complexity values independent of design. Does the reuser stay away from these modules, or take advantage of the greater payoff that comes from not having to redevelop complex code?

Table 22 lists the reusability assessment methods presented in this chapter. From the table we see that nearly all of the methods focus on attributes specific to the source code of the module. We start by looking at empirical methods, all of which we classify as module-oriented.

❖ EMPIRICAL METHODS

The following methods primarily use objective, quantifiable attributes of software as the basis for a reusability metric. Most use module-oriented attributes, but the methods used to interpret the attributes vary greatly.

PRIETO-DIAZ AND FREEMAN

In their landmark paper on faceted classification, Prieto-Diaz and Freeman identify five program attributes and associated metrics for evaluating reusability [115]. Their process model encourages white-box reuse and consists of finding candidate reusable modules, evaluating each, deciding which module the programmer can modify most easily, then adapting the module. In this model they identify four module-oriented metrics and a fifth metric used to modify the first four. The following list shows the five metrics and gives a description of each:

TABLE 22 *Reusability Metric Summary*

Method	E	Q	M	C
Prieto-Diaz and Freeman	✓		✓	
Selby	✓		✓	
Chen and Lee	✓		✓	
Caldiera and Basili	✓		✓	
REBOOT (reusability assessment)	✓		✓	
Hislop	✓		✓	
Boetticher and Eichmann	✓		✓	
Torres and Samadzadeh	✓		✓	
Mayobre	✓		✓	
NATO (metrics)	✓		✓	
Army (metrics)	✓		✓	
STARS		✓	✓	
U. Maryland		✓	✓	
NATO (guidelines)		✓	✓	
Army (guidelines)		✓	✓	
IBM		✓		✓
REBOOT (component quality)		✓		✓
Khairuddin and Key		✓		✓

NOTE:
E = Empirical
Q = Qualitative
M = Module-oriented
C = Component-oriented

1. **Program size.** Reuse depends on a small module size, as indicated by lines of source code.

2. **Program structure.** Reuse depends on a simple program structure, as indicated by fewer links to other modules (low coupling) and low cyclomatic complexity.

3. **Program documentation.** Reuse depends on excellent documentation, as indicated by a subjective overall rating on a scale of 1 to 10.

4. **Programming language.** Reuse depends on programming language to the extent that it helps to reuse a module written in the same programming language. If a reusable module in the same language does not exist, the degree of similarity between the target language and the one used in the module affects the difficulty of modifying the module to meet the new requirement.

5. **Reuse experience.** The experience of the reuser in the programming language and in the application domain affects the previous metrics because every programmer views a module from a different perspective. For example, programmers will have different views of what constitutes a "small" module, depending on their background. This fifth metric serves to modify the values of the other metrics.

SELBY

Selby provides a module-oriented, statistical study of reusability characteristics of software using data from a NASA software environment [131]. NASA used the environment to develop ground support software in FORTRAN for controlling unmanned spacecraft. To derive measures of reusability, Selby looked at instances where reuse succeeded and tried to determine *why.* His study provides empirical evidence based on the contributions of a wide range of code characteristics. The study statistically[12] validated most of the following findings at the .05 level of confidence, showing that most modules could be reused without modification:

- Have a smaller size, generally less than 140 source statements
- Have simple interfaces
- Have few calls to other modules (low coupling)
- Have more calls to low-level system and utility functions
- Have fewer input–output parameters
- Have less human interaction (user interface)
- Have good documentation, as shown by the comment-to-source statement ratio
- Have experienced few design changes during implementation
- Took less effort to design and build
- Have more assignment statements than logic statements per source statement
- Do not necessarily have low code complexity
- Do not depend on project size

REBOOT REUSABILITY ASSESSMENT

The ESPIRIT-2 project called REBOOT (Reuse Based on Object-Oriented Techniques) developed a taxonomy of reusability attributes. As part of the taxonomy, they list four

---

[12] Using nonparametric analysis-of-variance (ANOVA) models with ranked data [129].

reusability factors, a list of criteria for each factor, and a set of metrics for each criterion [73, 74]. Although some of the metrics depend on subjective items such as checklists, we can compute many of the metrics directly from the code, such as complexity, fan-in/out, and the comment-to-source-code ratio. This makes this method primarily a module-oriented, empirical metric. To complete the assessment, the analyst combines the individual metric values into an overall value for reusability. The following list defines the four reusability factors; Table 23 gives the criteria and metrics for each factor.

- **Portability.** The ease with which someone can transfer the software from one computer system to another. Criteria include:

  Modularity
  Environment independence

- **Flexibility.** The number of choices a programmer has in determining the use of the component; also referred to as "generality." Criteria include:

  Generality
  Modularity

- **Understandability.** The ease with which a programmer can understand the component. Criteria include:

  Code complexity
  Self-descriptiveness
  Documentation quality
  Component complexity

- **Confidence.** The subjective probability that a component will perform without failure over a specified time in a new environment. Criteria include:

  Component complexity
  Observed reliability
  Error tolerance

The reusability factors, criteria, and metrics interrelate as shown in Figure 13. We can arrive at a single value for the reusability by normalizing all metrics to a value in the interval 0–1 and taking the average:

$$Reusability = \frac{\sum_{i=1}^{n} (w_i \times Metric_i)}{\left(\sum_{i=1}^{n} w_j\right)}$$

where w_j describes the relative importance of each metric. Because REBOOT recognizes that the importance of a metric may change from site to site, the REBOOT metric allows the analyst to change these weights to most closely align with local

TABLE 23 *REBOOT Reusability Metrics for the Four Reusability Factors*

Criteria	Metric
Generality	Generality checklist
Modularity	Code/number of methods
Environment independence	Machine-dependent code/executable code
	System-dependent code/executable code
Code complexity	Cyclomatic complexity
Self-descriptiveness	Comments/source code
	Self-descriptiveness checklist
Documentation quality	Documentation/source code
	Documentation checklist
Component complexity	Fan-in, fan-out
	Cyclomatic complexity
Reliability	Total number of tests
	Number of observed errors
Error tolerance	Error tolerance checklist

priorities. Using this approach and a survey of 29 software developers in Europe, the REBOOT analysis shows the importance of understandability, reliability, and ease of porting the component to another environment [133].

OTHER EMPIRICAL METHODS

Researchers have experimented with many empirical methods, many of them taking very interesting or academic approaches. These range from training neural networks to identify components considered reusable by software engineering experts to using software originally intended to identify students who turn in the same programs on class projects. We now present some of these methods to illustrate the wide range of approaches we have seen regarding empirical measurement of reusability.

Chen and Lee

Although Selby's evidence did not find a statistically significant correlation between module complexity and reusability, other studies show such a link. In one example, Chen and Lee developed about 130 reusable C++ classes and used these classes in a controlled experiment to relate the level of reuse in a program to software productivity and quality [26]. In contrast to Selby, who worked with professional programmers, Chen and Lee's experiment involved 19 students who had to design and implement a small database system. Chen and Lee collected software metrics on Halstead size, program volume, program level, estimated difficulty, and effort, as well as

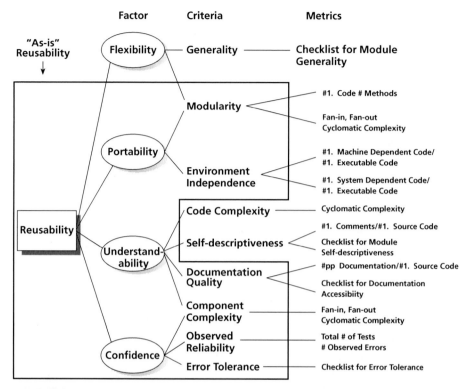

| Factor | Criteria | Metrics |

"As-is" Reusability

Flexibility — Generality ——————— Checklist for Module Generality

Modularity
— #1. Code # Methods
— Fan-in, Fan-out Cyclomatic Complexity

Portability

Environment Independence
— #1. Machine Dependent Code/ #1. Executable Code
— #1. System Dependent Code/ #1. Executable Code

Code Complexity ——————— Cyclomatic Complexity

Reusability

Understandability

Self-descriptiveness
— #1. Comments/#1. Source Code
— Checklist for Module Self-descriptiveness

Documentation Quality
— #pp Documentation/#1. Source Code
— Checklist for Documentation Accessibiity

Component Complexity
— Fan-in, Fan-out Cyclomatic Complexity

Observed Reliability
— Total # of Tests
— # Observed Errors

Confidence

Error Tolerance ——————— Checklist for Error Tolerance

FIGURE 13 *The REBOOT Reusability Factors, Criteria, and Metrics*

McCabe complexity and the Dunsmore live variable and variable span metrics [29]. They found that the lower the values for these complexity metrics, the higher the programmer productivity.

Caldiera and Basili

Caldiera and Basili [22] state that basic reusability attributes depend on (1) component costs, (2) quality, and (3) usefulness. The last attribute makes this model one of the few that addresses the effects of the environment on the reusability of an individual component. Taken together, the three attributes include many factors, such as correctness, readability, testability, ease of modification, and performance. Caldiera and Basili acknowledge that we cannot directly measure or predict most of these factors. Therefore, the paper proposes four candidate measures of reusability based largely on the McCabe and Halstead metrics. This module-oriented, empirical approach has an advantage in that tools can automatically calculate all of the four metrics and a range of values for each:

1. **Halstead's program volume.** A module must contain enough function to justify the costs of retrieving and integrating it, but not so much function as to jeopardize quality.

2. **McCabe's cyclomatic complexity.** Like Halstead's volume, the acceptable values for the McCabe metric must balance cost and quality.

3. **Regularity.** Regularity measures the readability and the redundancy of a module implementation by comparing the actual versus estimated values of Halstead's two length metrics. A clearly written module will have an actual Halstead length close to its theoretical Halstead length.

4. **Reuse frequency.** Reuse frequency indicates the proven usefulness of a module and comes from the number of static calls to the module.

The paper continues by calculating these four metrics for software in nine example systems, and noting that the four metrics show a high degree of statistical independence.

Hislop

Hislop discusses three approaches to evaluating software: (1) function, (2) form, and (3) similarity [63]. Evaluating software on *function* helps in selecting components based on what the component does. In fact, many reusable software collections use a hierarchical organization based on function. The second approach, *form*, characterizes the software based on observable characteristics such as size or structure. This approach lends itself well to code analysis tools that report on numbers of source statements or code complexity. The third approach, *similarity*, compares and groups modules according to shared attributes.

Hislop's work uses ideas drawn from plagiarism detection, where instructors seek to identify cases of students "reusing" each other's programs. The plagiarism analysis also helps in the study of reusability in a number of ways. First, a tool can identify potentially reusable modules in existing software by finding modules with a similarity metric close to those of successfully reused modules. Second, identifying groups of similar modules can help in domain analysis by showing opportunities for reuse. Third, the method can help automate reuse metrics by locating instances of informal reuse with or without modification.

Hislop's prototype tool, *SoftKin*, consists of a data collector and a data analyzer. The collector parses the software and calculates measures of form for each module. The analyzer computes the similarity measures based on a variety of form metrics such as McCabe complexity and structure profile metrics. This makes Hislop's method a module-oriented, empirical metric.

Boetticher and Eichmann

Recognizing the difficulty of defining what humans seem to accept as an intuitive notion of reusability, Boetticher and Eichmann take an alternative approach to reusability metrics. They base their work on the training of neural networks to mimic a set of human evaluators [16, 17]. They conducted experiments that varied several neural network configurations and each network's ability to match the output provided by a group of four humans. Using an Ada repository, the study used commercial metric tools to generate more than 250 code parameters with the goal of determining the best possible association between the parameters and the human assessments.

The input parameter selection contained code parameters representing module complexity, adaptability, and coupling. The experiment proceeded in three phases, using input parameters significant in *black-box* reuse (reuse without modification), *white-box* reuse (reuse with modification), and what they call *grey-box* reuse (a combination of black-box and white-box reuse). Black-box parameters included source statements, physical size, file size, and number of inputs/outputs. White-box parameters included Halstead volume, cyclomatic complexity, coupling, and size. Grey-box metrics combined the black-box and white-box inputs.

The experiment strove for a best fit through sensitivity analysis on parameters selected for the training vectors, the neural network configuration, and extent of network training. Although the black-box and white-box results showed little correlation with the expected outputs (.18 and .57, respectively), the grey box results correlated very well (.86) with the expert ratings. The experiment concluded that neural networks could serve as an economical, automatic tool to generate reusability rankings of software. We classify this method as module-oriented and empirically based.

Torres and Samadzadeh

Torres and Samadzadeh conducted a study to determine if information theory metrics and reusability metrics correlate [139]. Information theory measures information content as the level of entropy in a system (entropy reflects the degree of uncertainty or unpredictability in a system). This study examined the effects of two information theory metrics, *entropy loading* and *control structure entropy*, on software reusability.

Entropy loading reflects the degree of interprocess communication. Since the amount of communication required between parts of any system drives entropy up, information theory seeks ways to reduce entropy by designing systems with minimal communication between subsystems. Applying this concept to software, the researchers measure the amount of communication required between modules and assign a value for entropy loading to each module. Entropy loading corresponds to the software engineering concepts of coupling and cohesion; programs that possess small values for entropy loading should also possess properties consistent with good program structure and reusability. *Control structure entropy* seeks to measure the complexity of a module's logic structure, as reflected by the number of *if–then* statements in the module. Like cyclomatic complexity, control structure entropy provides a value for module complexity. The emphasis on code structures makes this method a module-oriented, empirical approach.

An experiment that calculated the two information theory metrics on six programs (three in Ada, three in C) found that high entropy loading (coupling) had a negative effect on reuse, while low control structure entropy (complexity) had a positive effect. The study concluded that there may be a relationship between information theory metrics and reusability metrics. Consequently, these metrics might help in selecting the optimum reuse case among different reuse candidates.

Mayobre

To help identify reusable workproducts in existing code, Mayobre describes a method called Code Reusability Analysis (CRA) [93]. CRA melds three reusability assessment methods and an economical estimation model to identify reusable components, resulting in a combination of automatic analysis and expert analysis to determine both technical reusability and economic value. First, CRA uses the Caldiera and Basili method. The second method, called the Domain Experience Based Component Identification Process (DEBCIP), depends on an extensive domain analysis of the problem area and uses a decision graph to help domain experts identify reusable components. The primary output of the DEBCIP provides an estimate of the expected number of reuse instances for the component.

The third method, called Variant Analysis Based Component Identification Process (VABCIP), also uses domain knowledge, but to a lesser degree. It uses cyclomatic complexity metrics to estimate the specification distance between the existing module and the required module, giving an estimate of the effort needed to modify the component. The last step of the reusability analysis consists of estimating the Component Return On Investment, a process consisting of comparing the estimated costs of reuse with the expected benefits.

A test of this method with 7–8 engineers and 40K source statements in the data communication domain showed a very high correlation of about 88% between the Caldiera and Basili metrics and expert analysis. The full CRA including VABCIP had better results, but took up to four weeks to complete and required a domain expert, a domain analyst, and a software engineer familiar with software metrics. We classify CRA as a module-oriented, empirical approach.

NATO

The NATO Standard for Software Reuse Procedures recommends tracking four metrics as indicators of software quality and reusability [98]. The metrics help in evaluating modules based primarily on statistics gathered through experience with the modules. This makes the NATO metrics a module-oriented, empirical method. The metrics include the following:

- **Number of inspections.** The number of times someone has considered the module for reuse.
- **Number of reuses.** The number of times someone actually has reused the module.
- **Complexity.** The complexity of the code, normally based on the McCabe complexity metric.
- **Number of problem reports.** The number of outstanding defects in the module.

These metrics give a rough estimate of the reusability of a component that can help eliminate unsuitable candidates for reuse. For example, potential reusers should look for components with a high number of prior reuses, but remain skeptical of components with a high number of inspections and few actual reuses. The standard recommends reusing components with low complexity values and fewer known defects.

U.S. Army Reuse Center

The Army Reuse Center (ARC) inspects all software submitted to the Defense Software Repository System (DSRS) [121]. As part of that inspection, each component undergoes a series of reusability evaluations [103]. The preliminary screening consists of coarse measures of module size in source statements, the estimated effort to reuse the component without modification, the estimated effort needed to develop a new component rather than reuse one, the estimated yearly maintenance effort, and the number of expected reuses of the component.

Following this screening, the ARC conducts several other assessments and tests. They calculate an initial and a final reusability metric using a commercially available Ada source code analysis tool. The initial analysis uses 31 metrics supplied by the tool; the final analysis uses a total of 150 metrics. This takes a module-oriented, empirical approach. Table 24 lists a subset of the 31 metrics used in the initial analysis by metric category, and gives the metric threshold values required by the ARC.

TABLE 24 *Partial List of ARC Reusability Metrics*

Category	Metric	Threshold value
Anomaly management	Normal_Loops	95%
	Constrained_Subtype	80%
	Constraint_Error	80%
	Constrained_Numerics	90%
	Constraint_Error	0%
	Program_Error	0%
	Storage_Error	0%
	Numeric_Error	0%
	User_Exception_Raised	100%
Independence	No_Missed_Closed	0%
	Fixed_Clause	100%
	No_Pragma_Pack	0%
	No_Machine_Code_Stmt	100%
	No_Impl_Dep_Pragmas	0%
	No_Impl_Dep_Attrs	0%

❖ QUALITATIVE METHODS

Because finding and agreeing upon a purely objective reusability metric often proves difficult, many organizations provide subjective (nonempirical) guidance on identifying or building reusable software. Good examples come from Edwards [35], Hollingsworth [61], Hooper and Chester [62], NATO [97], and the ARC [121]. These guidelines help ameliorate the problem of not knowing *exactly* how to define reusability by substituting an intuitive description of what a reusable component ought to look like. The guidelines range in content from general discussions about designing for reuse to very detailed rules and specific design points for particular languages such as Ada [61, 132]. Usually module-oriented, the guidelines cover points such as formatting and style requirements. Although guidelines primarily help developers *design for reuse* or *build for reuse*, organizations may develop reusability metrics based on how well a component meets the published standard.

Rather than expand on the many available guidelines, this section presents some general "reusability" attributes and two examples showing how these attributes translate to reusability principles. Finally, this section ends with an example of a component-oriented approach.

GENERAL REUSABILITY ATTRIBUTES

Most sets of reusability guidelines have a lot in common and vary only in the code-specific rules and level of detail. In general, the guidelines reflect the same software characteristics as those promoted by good software engineering principles [114]. This emphasizes the fact that reuse requires a focus on the basic problem of good software design and development. Table 25 gives a high-level summary of these software engineering concepts as seen by the Software Technology for Adaptable, Reliable Systems (STARS) Program [134].

The application of these abstract concepts will in large part determine their reuse success. In situations where one team provides shared software to the rest of a project, the modules this team builds need to be general enough for multiple uses, with enough supporting information to make the modules easily useful. Simply put, if the team developing the modules does not meet their customers' needs, their customers will not use the modules. The reuse team must make the modules general by carefully examining each customer requirement and abstracting the necessary detail.

TABLE 25 *General Attributes of Reusable Software*

Attribute	*Description*
Ease of understanding	The component has thorough documentation, including self-documenting code and in-line comments.
Functional completeness	The component has all the required operations for the current requirement and any reasonable future requirements.
Reliability	The component consistently performs the advertised function without error and passes repeated tests across various hardware and operating systems.
Good error and exception handling	The component isolates, documents, and handles errors consistently. It also provides a variety of options for error response.
Information hiding	The component hides implementation details from the user, for example, internal variables and their representation. It also clearly defines the interfaces to other operations and data.
High cohesion and low coupling	The component does a specific, isolated function with minimal external dependencies.
Portability	The component does not depend on unique hardware or operating system services.

IBM REUSABILITY GUIDELINES

IBM assesses reusability using a number of criteria that extend well beyond the module source code. IBM's method stresses that for a developer to efficiently use a software module, the developer needs to have access to other information such as design documents, integration instructions, test cases, and legal information [106]. This makes the IBM method a component-oriented, qualitative approach to reusability. Table 26 contains a listing of the kinds of supporting information IBM provides to potential reusers. A component receives one of three quality ratings, based in part on the completeness and quality of the information supporting the reusable module.

KHAIRUDDIN AND KEY

Khairuddin and Key have examined the general attributes of reusability and formed these attributes into a reusability model [76]. These attributes span the fields of quality, maintainability, portability, and other areas that intuitively lead to more reusable software. Figure 14 depicts this reusability attributes model. Khairuddin and Key

TABLE 26 *Information Helpful When Reusing Software*

Attribute	Description
Abstract	Provides a clear, concise description of the component.
Change history	Describes changes to the code, who made them, the date of the changes, and why.
Dependencies	Describes prerequisite software and other software the component uses.
Design	Describes the internal design of the code and major design decisions.
Interfaces	Describes all inputs, outputs, operations, exceptions, and any other side effects visible to the reuser.
Legal	Provides a summary of legal information and restrictions, such as license and copyright information.
Performance	Describes the time requirements, space requirements, and any performance considerations of the algorithm.
Restrictions	Lists any situations that limit the usability of the component, such as nonstandard compiler options and known side effects.
Sample	Provides a usage scenario showing how the component applies to a specific problem.
Test	Contains information about the test history, procedures, results, and test cases.
Usage	Provides helpful information on how to integrate the component.

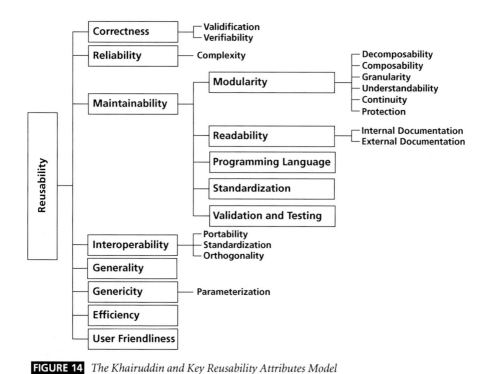

FIGURE 14 *The Khairuddin and Key Reusability Attributes Model*

propose using the model to develop a metric that can quantify a reusability index for components and thereby, for example, qualify the component for admission to a reuse library. The authors do not attempt to develop actual metrics for the attributes, making this a qualitative model. However, like the IBM model, Khairuddin and Key include aspects external to a component such as the readability of its supporting documentation and the "user-friendliness" of the component.

OTHER QUALITATIVE METHODS

We mention the following qualitative methods because of their influence on reusability. The 3C model has affected reusability researchers since its introduction, whereas the University of Maryland approaches represent findings from several different projects. Finally, the REBOOT qualification criteria make a good companion to the REBOOT empirical reusability assessment model.

The 3C model

The name of the "3C model" of reusable software components comes from its three constituent design points [142]:

1. **Concept:** What abstraction the component represents.

2. **Content:** How the component implements the abstraction.

3. **Context:** The environment in which the component operates.

The concept of a component relates to its specification or interface; it gives a black-box perspective of the component's function. The content relates to the actual algorithm, or code, that implements the function abstracted by the concept. The context refers to those parts of the environment that affect the use of the component; in other words, the context defines the component's dependencies when used in another application.

The 3C model seeks to isolate concept, content, and context-specific dependencies from each other during the design and implementation of a module. By building a clear boundary between each, a reuser can modify one without affecting the others. For example, several module implementations may exist to serve the same interface, thereby allowing the reuser to select the best implementation to meet specific constraints or performance criteria. Successful implementation of the 3C model would allow developers to treat modules as "software integrated circuits" by plugging them into sockets in an application framework. Because the 3C model focuses on general aspects of module design, we classify it as a module-oriented, qualitative reusability method.

University of Maryland

Two example sets of coding guidelines to increase the reusability of Ada modules resulted from a set of reuse-related projects at the University of Maryland [4, 11]. These guidelines fall into two categories: those based on data binding, and those based on transformation. Data binding measures the strength of data coupling between modules. Transformation formally quantifies the number and types of modifications required to adapt a module into something reusable. The approaches take a module-oriented, qualitative approach to reusability.

The University of Maryland approaches stress that component reusability corresponds directly to the estimated effort required to modify a component for use in a new context. Although many complicated factors contribute to the actual effort required to modify a component, they have observed that an initial estimate of the modification effort using an ordinal scale can serve as a reusability measure [5]. Their reusability guidelines therefore seek to reduce the modification effort. By writing modules to reduce data binding dependencies and the number of expected changes required, a programmer can develop more reusable modules. The following example guidelines reflect software engineering principles applied to Ada:

Reuse guidelines based on data bindings:

- Avoid multiple-level nesting in language constructs.
- Minimize use of the "use" clause.
- The interfaces of the subprograms should use the appropriate abstraction for the parameters passed in and out.
- Components should not interact with their outer environment.
- Appropriate use of packaging could greatly enhance reusability.

Reuse guidelines based on dependencies:

- Avoid direct access into record components except in the same declarative region as the record type declaration.
- Minimize nonlocal access to array components.
- Keep direct access to data structures local to their declarations.
- Avoid the use of literal values except as constant value assignments.
- Avoid mingling resources with application-specific contexts.
- Keep interfaces abstract.

REBOOT qualification criteria

In addition to the REBOOT empirical reusability assessment, REBOOT also produced a model for assessing the information related to a reusable module. In an approach similar to that used at IBM, the REBOOT *qualification criterion* considers a reusable component to consist not only of the actual module, but also of its supporting documentation [125]. Reusable components can range from high-level architectures and designs for systems to low-level building blocks of code. A reusable code component does not consist solely of source code, but also includes *parts* containing design structures, specifications, and documentation. In the REBOOT model, a reusable component contains the following parts:

1. Parts that correspond to the *development* phase, consisting of information directly related to the component, such as source code files, analysis, designs, test cases, and documents containing information useful to reusers of the component.

2. An *administrative* part containing information concerning the life of the component (i.e., creation date, author, versions).

3. A *historical* part containing summary information regarding the development history of the component. This includes the methodology and tools used to develop the component, as well as information that may assist the reuser in adapting the component.

4. A *classification* part containing the classifiers and their values which REBOOT uses to store, search for, and retrieve the components from the REBOOT reuse repository.

REBOOT selected these aggregations of parts to support different user views of the component. For example, a programmer would work primarily with the parts related to *development*, whereas the REBOOT librarian would work almost exclusively with the *classification* part.

❖ A COMMON MODEL FOR REUSABILITY

The wide range of approaches that we have presented illustrates the diversity of ideas that come forward when discussing software reusability. We examined the approaches and their results in order to identify the attributes that tended to contribute the most to what the researchers considered a "reusable component." We see that most empirical methods take a module-oriented approach, since modules provide many easily measurable attributes. Of these attributes, the following appear common to most of the empirical methods:

1. Reusable modules have low module complexity.

2. Reusable modules have good documentation (a high number of nonblank comment lines).

3. Reusable modules have few external dependencies (low fan-in and fan-out, few input and output parameters).

4. Reusable modules have proven reliability (thorough testing and low error rates).

The qualitative methods vary in their application of software engineering principles, code-specific implementation issues, and level of detail. When they assign a reusability value to a module, they typically base the value on a subjective assessment of how well a module complies with a set of guidelines. While a subjective assessment does not qualify as a true metric, it does indicate how a developer might perceive a module's "reusability." Component-oriented approaches not only specify code standards, but also list required supporting information that can help a developer effectively reuse a component.

❖ DOMAIN CONSIDERATIONS

Tracz observed that for programmers to reuse software, they must first find it *useful* [141]. In some sense, researchers have fully explored most traditional methods of measuring reusability: complexity, module size, interface characteristics, etc. However, although many recognize the importance of the problem *domain* to reuse, few have linked this effect to the ultimate "usefulness" of a component.

The usefulness of a component depends as much on the framework in which it fits as it does on internal characteristics of the component. Most of the research in software reusability has examined domain-independent software, as explained in "Expected Levels of Reuse" on page 5. The research focuses on this software because these generally low-level utilities appear in many applications and researchers consequently classify it as "reusable." However, the research must also consider domain-specific software, the use of which depends as much on the software it works with as it does on its own internal attributes. Reusing domain-independent software will only bring limited benefits. The real benefits of reuse occur following:

1. an analysis of the problem domain,
2. capturing the domain using appropriate domain models,
3. constructing a Domain-Specific Software Architecture (DSSA), and
4. building components for use in the architecture.

Although low coupling, high cohesiveness, modularity, etc., give a general idea of the ease of use of a component, they cannot, by themselves, provide a measure of reusability for all software. In fact, a study intended to establish a correlation between empirical software metrics and qualitative ("perceived") measures of reusability found no linear relationship between ease of use and reusability [128]. Reusability seems to come more from adhering to a software architecture, to a DSSA, and to the above software engineering principles. With the exception of the 3C model and the work by Mayobre, the preceding methods do not include any software architecture or domain characteristics. The input parameters come from observable or readily obtainable data about the software component. However, experience and research shows that a domain's size, stability, and maturity have a dominant effect on how many times we can actually use a component [25, 67]. If the reusability of a component depends on *context*, then reusability metrics must also include characteristics about the software architecture, domain, and related environment.

APPLYING METRIC THEORY

The fact remains that most published work in software metrics, including reusability metrics, does not follow the important rules of measurement theory. We do not want to elaborate on the details of that theory here. However, with regard to reusability metrics, we can informally say that any number we assign to a component's reusability must preserve the intuitive understanding and observations we make about that component. This understanding leads us to put a value on the metric. More formally, if we observe component A as less reusable than component B, then our reusability measurement, M, must preserve $M(A) < M(B)$.

The first problem in metric theory comes from our trying to put an empirical value on a poorly understood attribute. To make matters worse, relations we define generally fall apart when we change contexts. We often find that a component we feel has very high reusability attributes in domain X and environment S has none of these characteristics in domain Y and environment T. Software engineers working in these two situations would never reach consensus on the reusability for this individual component. This makes the search for a general reusability metric difficult or impossible for the same reasons Fenton discusses regarding the search for a general software complexity metric [42].

Metric theory tells us that we can look for metrics that assign an empirical value to specific *attributes* or *views* of reusability, but not an overall reusability rating. Furthermore, if research truly reveals that *context* affects our view of a component's reusability as much as the component's internal attributes, then we may some day find a metric M that maps the tuple (*internal attributes, domain attributes, environment attributes*) to M. In other words, we may develop a general reusability metric that includes attributes from the domain and environment as well as the individual component.

❖ CONCLUSION

Although reusability guidelines and module-oriented metrics provide an intuitive feel for *attributes* that lead to the reusability of a component, they have not yet been proved to reflect a component's reuse potential. Until researchers can agree on this issue, we will not develop a general metric. Existing techniques show a wide range of ways to address this problem, ranging from empirical to qualitative methods. So far, the results mostly indicate a need to first define a suitable scope for future research. This scope should include the affects of *software architecture, domain,* and *environment* when we talk about measuring the "reusability" of individual components. We conclude with the key observation that:

> *Software reusability depends on attributes from the environment as well as individual components.*

❖ 8 ❖

Metrics for Reuse Libraries

This book focuses on defining reuse from a metrics point of view, measuring reuse levels, and assessing the benefits of reuse. However, for the past decade most of the attention in the field of software reuse has centered on reuse libraries. Research has explored means of efficiently classifying, storing, and retrieving components; this focus has caused many organizations to build some form of reuse repository or reuse library tool. In this chapter we make some concise recommendations on metrics that an organization can use in conjunction with their Reusable Software Library (RSL).

❖ RECOMMENDED METRICS

Because many organizations have started to use World Wide Web (WWW) servers to implement RSLs, they have access to a wide range of data about the RSL [109]. The RSL librarian simply needs to configure the WWW server to automatically collect information on its own use. However, what can this data tell us? In addition to recommending metrics, this section tells how to interpret the metrics for the purpose of both evaluating and improving the library.

The following metrics can help assess the benefits derived from an RSL. Note that before using data collected by an RSL, we need to filter out usage data caused by the librarian. Valid metrics come from users of the library, not from library maintenance.

- **Number of accesses to the RSL.** WWW-based libraries and most commercial RSLs can provide this data automatically and easily. The number of RSL accesses indicates how much people actually use the RSL. We find trend data (number of accesses per month) especially helpful. Trends showing increasing usage confirm RSL success, whereas trends showing decreasing usage indicate a need for some kind of action. In the latter case, we might consider providing different components or generating more publicity for the library.

A good librarian can help identify actions for improvement by talking with library users. If the usage data contains the *userids* or Internet Protocol (IP) addresses of users, the librarian can follow up by contacting organizations that access the RSL. The librarian should ask if the organization found what they needed and if they need any other kinds of components or other assistance. Library users provide the best ideas for making the RSL mechanism and its contents better.

- **The number of accesses per component.** We want to find the number of times that potential reusers have examined each individual component in the RSL. This metric can tell several things. First, it tells us what components the RSL users find most interesting for potential reuse. We can use this information to decide if our organization needs to invest in more components in the same functional area. Second, if the data tell how many times people actually retrieved the component, then we can start to estimate benefits of the RSL.

  If the data show that a component has had many accesses but few retrievals, then we may have a problem with the component. The component appeals to potential reusers; it may "look good," have an interesting name, or fall into an important domain. However, although people seem to *need* the component, the documentation, comments, reliability, or some other factor precludes its usability. We need to take a closer look at components that fall into this category.

- **Source Instructions Reused by Others (SIRBO).** Most commercial RSL tools cannot track what happens to a component after a potential reuser extracts the component from the RSL. However, the real value of an RSL comes from how many times people actually *used* the components. Because an RSL supplies reusable components in the same way as a organization that produces software for reuse, we can calculate a SIRBO for the RSL as explained in "Reuse Value Added" on page 79. The RSL's SIRBO represents the total LOC that users of the RSL did not have to write because the RSL contained a component they could reuse.

  If the librarian does not have an automated way to obtain SIRBO data through the RSL tool, software configuration management tool, etc., then the librarian may have to do this task manually. The librarian should follow up via electronic mail or phone with individuals who have extracted components from the repository. The librarian needs to ask if the organizations actually integrated the components that they extracted from the RSL into their applications. If the organization reused the component, then the size of the component, in lines of code, contributes to the SIRBO of the RSL.

- **RSL ROI.** Whereas the SIRBO tells us how much RSL software organizations reuse, we really want to know the economic value of the reuse. After finding the SIRBO, we use it to build our business case for the RSL. We do this using the same method that we used with the *Project ROI* metric from "A Reuse Metric Starter Set" on page 97. To calculate the RSL ROI, simply (1) substitute $RSI = SIRBO$ in the Reuse Cost Avoided (RCA) metric, and (2) substitute the costs to maintain the RSL, $RSL_{costs,}$ in place of *Additional Development Costs (ADC)*. Costs to maintain the RSL will include labor costs for the librarian, costs of capital for equipment used to store the RSL, and fees for commercial reusable software collections that the organization licenses for distribution via the RSL.

Example: Last year our RSL supplied Component A (consisting of 4800 LOC) to one organization, Component B (1273 LOC) to seven organizations, and Component C (211 LOC) to one organization. We spent approximately $85K in labor and $2K in computer costs to support the RSL for the year. We want to develop a business case for continued funding of the RSL for the upcoming year.

First, we calculate the SIRBO for the RSL as:

$$SIRBO = \sum (LOC\ per\ part) \times (Organizations\ using\ the\ part)$$

$$= (4800\ LOC \times 1\ org) + (1273\ LOC \times 7\ orgs) + (211\ LOC \times 1\ org)$$

$$= 13{,}922\ LOC$$

Second, we calculate the RCA for the RSL using the default values for the historical data that we have used throughout this book:

$$DCA = SIRBO \times (1 - RCR) \times New\ code\ cost$$

$$= 13{,}922\ LOC \times (1 - 0.2) \times \$100\ per\ line$$

$$= 13{,}922\ LOC \times .8 \times \$100\ per\ line$$

$$= \$1{,}113{,}760$$

$$SCA = SIRBO \times Error\ rate \times Error\ cost$$

$$= 13{,}922\ LOC \times 1\ errors\ per\ KLOC \times \$10K\ per\ error$$

$$= \$139{,}220$$

For an RCA due to the RSL of:

$$RCA = Development\ Cost\ Avoidance\ +\ Service\ Cost\ Avoidance$$

$$= \$1,113,760 + \$139,220$$

$$= \$1,252,980$$

The total cost to maintain the RSL consists of labor and computer costs, so RSL_{costs} = \$85K + \$2K = \$87K. This results in an ROI for the RSL of:

$$RSL\ ROI = RCA - RSL_{costs}$$

$$= \$1,252,980 - \$87,000$$

$$= \$1,165,980$$

Last year's *RSL ROI* = \$1,165,980 from an investment of \$87K supports your business case for the RSL.

Obtaining a documented list of actual component reuses in terms of the SIRBO and assigning a value to those reuses using the RSL ROI have proven the most informative and useful of all library metrics. We find this data very important for future funding and support of an RSL.

❖ REUSE LIBRARY EFFICIENCY

A small collection of useful components is more valuable than a large reuse library containing many useless components. To emphasize this, the Software Productivity Consortium developed an interesting metric to indicate the usefulness of an RSL on an application [32].

The library efficiency metric shows how well the reuse library contributed to the development of an application. The metric represents the percentage of an application using software from the library relative to the total amount of software contained in the library:

$$Library\ Efficiency = E = \frac{S_R}{S_L}$$

Where:

S_R = the size (in LOC) of the reused code in the application
S_L = the size (in LOC) of the reused code in the reuse library.

For small, domain-specific libraries, the value of E for an application in the domain may approach or even equal 1. This would represent the situation where the application used all the software in the reuse library.

Example: At McDonnell Douglas Aerospace, engineers developed a domain-specific library for use on the NASA Advanced Simulation Development System (ASDS) [53]. ASDS propagates discrete events to create non-real-time trajectory and vehicle simulations, although the design permits simulating a wide range of activities. McDonnell Douglas developed the original library in Ada and have since implemented a C version for use on the space shuttle. The total library consists of only 299 Ada modules and 55 C modules, for a total of 39.4K LOC and 21.7K LOC, respectively. However, experiences with the ASDS library show that these modules typically provide 50–90% of the total simulation software. A developer reuses almost every module in a black-box fashion; when a developer must reengineer modules it typically involves less than 10% of the simulation. In five recent simulations, McDonnell Douglas determined that three of the simulations used over 70% of the code in the ASDS library, and the remaining two simulations used over 50% of the code in the library. This results in an ASDS *Library Efficiency* = 70% and a *Library Efficiency* = 50%.

An organization can also use this metric to show how much organizations actually reuse the contents of the RSL. The example just given shows a small and "efficient" domain-specific RSL. On the other hand, many large corporations and government agencies sponsor reuse libraries that contain extremely large numbers of components. We can obtain a value for the library efficiency metric by setting S_R equal to the total amount of software extracted from the library and actually reused on projects. In these cases the values for E will probably equal very small fractions, indicating a very inefficient RSL. When faced with this situation, the organization that owns the RSL must make a business decision to justify the cost of cataloging, storing, and maintaining the high proportion of unused components. For example, the GTE Corporation shrunk the number of reusable components in its RSL from 190 components in 1988 to 128 components in 1990 by deleting unused components [116].

❖ CONCLUSION

This chapter presented some recommended metrics for evaluating and improving the effectiveness of an organization's RSL. As with other reuse metrics, showing the benefit of the RSL in financial terms using the RSL ROI can make a very powerful business case for the RSL. We conclude by noting that this chapter did not include one very popular RSL metric: one that measures the *total number of components in the RSL*.

A much-misunderstood and almost worthless metric, the *total number of components in the RSL* has nonetheless been widely publicized by owners of large reuse libraries. Unfortunately, the number of components in an RSL may have nothing to do with the total number of *useful* components in the RSL [113].

We do not recommend this metric. Almost every library in the past 10 years has made the mistake of using this metric as a measure of success. As a result, these RSLs have often become full of almost worthless software. In contrast, the most successful libraries contain relatively small collections of 100–250 components; in rare cases they contain up to 1000 components. Nonetheless, these small RSLs tend to enjoy high levels of reuse because a lot of thought (domain analysis) went into making these components usable within a given application area (domain).

❖ **9** ❖

Measuring Reuse Across the Life Cycle

Most current reuse measurement models focus on quantifying the level of software, i.e., code reused on a given project. One reason for this is the relative ease of quantifying the amount of code in a given product. A second, perhaps more critical, reason is the difficulty of completely understanding the issues behind reuse in other phases of the life cycle, such as requirements [99], design [16], information [148], and test cases [130]. Future work needs to describe a method to quantify the total amount of cross-life-cycle reuse on a project. Until we have practical and reliable methods of understanding and quantifying the issues in each phase of software development, we will depend on our current code reuse models to reflect the overall level of reuse in our systems [107].

To develop a reuse level metric that spans the entire software life cycle, we must develop a method of measuring reuse in each phase. The phases of the life cycle may include the reuse of requirements specifications, designs, user documentation, and other products related to the project. Since code really only accounts for about 20% of the effort in software development [50], it seems misleading to claim reuse levels on a product based solely on the amount of reused source code.

❖ LOC WORKS AS AN OVERALL INDICATOR

Unfortunately, we do not currently have a means to determine the total reuse on a product based on reuse in each of the life cycle stages. We know that where code reuse takes place, reuse of designs, test cases, and documentation has probably also taken place. In fact, domain analysis and engineering provides a very powerful method for reusing all these work products at the same time. When we construct systems that conform with the software architecture that we have constructed for our domain, we measure high levels of reuse based on code. However, although our investment in building this architecture manifests itself in reused components that we can readily

139

measure, it also includes reuse of all the requirements, design, analysis, and other work surrounding the individual components.

This "inclusion effect" of reusing subsequent life-cycle products motivates us to reuse early in the life cycle to obtain the most value from our reused parts [18]. Because of this effect, until we develop a comprehensive system of measuring and combining reuse in each phase of the software development life cycle, our metrics for level of code reuse will serve to approximate the total amount of reuse across the life cycle. This position is based on the plethora of evidence showing that, despite their shortcomings, LOC not only serve as a good indicator of overall productivity in code, but also provide a good secondary indicator of work done in other phases [136].

❖ A METHOD TO QUANTIFY TOTAL LIFE-CYCLE REUSE

While we use code reuse metrics as an overall product indicator, we can work towards realizing the following model of *Life-Cycle Reuse%*. Note that we use the *Reuse%* symbol, indicating a well-defined counting method. Observations show reuse percent as the most widely used and reported reuse metric. Measuring reuse levels with percents has an advantage in that managers can easily gather data for, calculate, and understand the metric. As with code, a cross-life-cycle approach must assume a systematic method of determining what to count (see Chapter 4, "Defining Reuse from a Metrics Point of View").

To implement a metric, we require a means of measuring reuse in each stage of the life cycle. A straightforward approach to measuring reuse in each phase would extend the approach currently used to measure reuse of code. We first need to determine the unit of granularity or work-product unit of interest at each stage. We might use the following units:

- **Requirements:** number of requirements, number of objects (functions, processes, data) in business models, number of major headings in requirements document.
- **Code:** lines of code, function points.
- **Design:** module design sheet, component specification, Program Design Language (PDL) statements, design objects from CASE tool.
- **Test:** test cases, test scripts.
- **Information Development:** words, tokens, paragraphs, pages.

Alternately, we can use a measure of *effort*, a unit common to all phases. For organizations with the ability to track or estimate effort, labor-months (LM) would serve as an excellent unit. *Cost* would also make a good candidate unit. However, we feel that LM will prove more reliable than cost because of variations in company-dependent finances, salaries, and because of international variables such as local currencies and exchange rates.

Observe that once we define the units to use at each phase and we put a process (and required tools) in place to track these units, we can determine the reuse percent for each phase. We base the *Reuse%* for each stage to represent the portion of units reused in that stage. Although we cannot generally do this today, some organizations have made progress in this area.

Example 1: Matra Cap Systemes measures design reuse as reuse of "design elements." A design element consists of a large-grained system object which normally results during the code phase in from 5 to 20 C++ classes. By tracking design elements, an organization can assign a reuse level to the design phase of their projects [60].

Example 2: Northern Telecom adopted the Poulin and Caruso reuse metrics with some modifications to allow for measuring reuse in areas other than code. Specifically, Northern Telecom uses "design units" as managed by their object-oriented design tool to define "design reuse." When an organization uses another organization's design units without modification, organizations at Northern Telecom count them towards their *Design Reuse%*.

Our approach assumes each life-cycle phase has well-defined boundaries (e.g., we can calculate a *Reuse%* for each phase). It also assumes that the software development process remains relatively stable (e.g., that we can model the total life-cycle as the sum of the activity in each of the individual phases). Although these assumptions may not hold for any given project, they allow us to develop a general equation for *Life-Cycle Reuse%*.

To achieve an overall *Life-Cycle Reuse%*, we determine the portion of total product effort expended in each phase of the life cycle. For post-mortem statistics, actual values will yield the best results, but for a general model we can use historical averages obtained from the organization product development office. For example, we might use the following life-cycle effort profile in our general model [50]:

- ◆ *Requirements Definition* takes 15% of the life cycle
- ◆ *Design* takes 15% of the life cycle
- ◆ *Code* takes 20% of the life cycle
- ◆ *Test* takes 30% of the life cycle
- ◆ *Information Development/Admin* takes 20% of the life cycle

Knowing the *Reuse%* in each phase and the relative effort expended in each phase, we can calculate the overall *Life-Cycle Reuse%* as follows:

$$Life\text{-}Cycle\ Reuse\% \ = \ \sum_{i=1}^{n} (Relative\ effort\ in\ Phase_i) \ \times \ (Reuse\%\ in\ Phase_i)$$

where n = number of phases in the life cycle.

Example: Total life-cycle reuse calculation.

Let the entire software development cycle for an organization consist of the five phases above, in the proportions given. Let the following situations determine the amount of reuse in each phase:

- *Requirements Definition*: 25% of requirements for the current system came from a similar system done last year for another customer.

- *Design*: 55% of the designs, mostly coming from the requirements reused in the previous phase, came straight out of the graphical CASE tool library used by the design department.

- *Code*: 35% of the code came unmodified from the organization's reuse subdirectory on the shared file system.

- *Test*: 25% of the test cases and drivers from other projects worked just fine without change.

- *Information Development/Admin*: 65% of the documentation, mostly from hypertext links to help files and user instructions, came from the Information Development (ID) database.

The *Life-Cycle Reuse%* would equal the sum of:

Reuse% in Requirements Definition: $.15 \times .25 \ = \ .038$
Reuse% in Design: $.15 \times .55 \ = \ .083$
Reuse% in Code: $.20 \times .35 \ = \ .07$
Reuse% in Test: $.30 \times .25 \ = \ .075$
Reuse% in Information Development/Admin: $.20 \times .65 \ = \ .13$

The total *Life-Cycle Reuse%* = 39.6%.

Unfortunately, this model does not really become practical until we can agree upon a standard method for measuring reuse in every life-cycle phase. Because we can currently only measure reuse in the coding phase, even if we achieve high levels of code reuse the overall life-cycle level of reuse cannot be a very high number. Using the life-cycle breakdown above, an impressive reuse level of 50% during coding only contributes $0.20 \times 50\% = 10\%$ to the total *Life-Cycle Reuse%*. This result seems to support the use of code reuse metrics as a general indicator of life-cycle reuse levels for the foreseeable future.

❖ CONCLUSION

In this chapter we developed a straightforward method for calculating the reuse level for all phases of the software life cycle. We call this level the *Life-Cycle Reuse%*. We calculated the *Life-Cycle Reuse%* by taking the sum of the levels of reuse in all phases of the life cycle after weighting the levels by the amount of effort required in each phase. With a little effort we can also develop a Cost Avoidance equation for the entire life cycle just as we did for RCA.

Because code takes only one portion of the life cycle, we saw that even high levels of code reuse will make a limited contribution to *Life-Cycle Reuse%*. The examples showed that in order to attain high levels of reuse across the life cycle, we will have to attain high levels of reuse in *every phase* of the life cycle.

Our efforts to quantify these reuse levels depend on having a way to quantify the work products we develop in each phase. We currently do not have standard units or methods for these work products. However, an abundance of evidence shows that the number of lines of code in a project corresponds to the total effort expended by the project; companies routinely use this observation in their business practices. We conclude that:

> **Lines of Code work as an overall indicator of reuse.**

This observation tells us that we can use the reuse levels we calculate using lines of code to approximate the total amount of reuse on a project. We expect to use LOC-based reuse levels until we find standard units and repeatable methods to measure our work-products in all life-cycle phases.

❖ 10 ❖

Conclusions and Future Directions

This book has illustrated the major issues in reuse metrics. Most importantly, it has defined a common method of counting software reuse and provided a recommended set of metrics to use for measuring an organization's reuse levels and corresponding financial benefits. We conclude the book by reviewing the key observations we have made through the book and then taking a look forward to areas open for future work.

❖ SUMMARY

Reuse metrics not only highlight the benefits of reuse, they can help projects "buy into" a reuse program. A simple, straightforward set of metrics allows organizations to do the following:

- ◆ Create their own business cases and see what reuse can do for them,
- ◆ Monitor their progress, and
- ◆ Increase the level of reuse on their projects.

Ultimately, support for the decision to reuse comes down to whether or not we have a favorable business case. This emphasizes our first key observation:

> **Business decisions drive reuse!**

If the expected benefits exceed the costs, then the organization has the motivation to reuse. However, to achieve real results we must *institutionalize reuse*; this takes more than a directive from the executive ranks. Institutionalizing reuse means:

- ◆ Fully integrating reuse into the software development cycle, and
- ◆ Making reuse "Business as Usual" for the organization.

Institutionalizing reuse and developing a BAU attitude require training, a dedicated, knowledgeable champion, and a process that every developer understands. Metrics can help an organization do this. Metrics help modify behavior by measuring and thereby focusing on what you want an organization to do. Management enforces change by emphasizing the metric, reporting it, and responding to the values of the metric. So if we want to succeed in reuse, we must remember this key observation:

> ### Reuse metrics can help you achieve your reuse goals.

The most significant issue in reuse metrics comes from the many different ways that organizations count reuse. Assigning a realistic reuse level and benefit due to reuse does not require much work *if you have trustworthy data*. However, Chapter 4, "Defining Reuse from a Metrics Point of View," shows that organizations have placed some pretty unconventional things under the banner of "reuse." Whether assessing a reuse report from someone else or setting up your own metrics, remember this key observation:

> ### No one defines what they count!

We cannot trust an experience report unless it explains what it counted as reuse. This book makes a significant contribution to reuse metrics by clearly defining a reuse counting method. We call software that complies with this method a *Reused Source Instruction (RSI)*.

At the center to the definition of RSI lies the key observation that:

> ### Organizational structure determines when reuse takes place!

Structured programming and software engineering taught us how to write good software. However, software engineering cannot teach us how to effectively apply our programming skills and coordinate efforts across large projects. This includes the systematic sharing of software outside of our own development organization. We call this *the boundary problem*. Organizations that avoid work by obtaining software from other places experience the benefits of reuse. "The Boundary Problem" on page 34 explained how counting the RSI starts by looking at software that has crossed these organizational or application boundaries.

Having a definition for reuse in the form of *RSI* helps guarantee uniformity and equity when reporting reuse results. Likewise, using the symbol *Reuse%* automatically conveys that we calculated the reuse level using the counting method defined for *RSI*.

Experience reports using *RSI* and *Reuse%* give a sense of consistency and a knowledge of what the report really shows.

Measuring reuse levels meets only our initial need for reuse metrics. Since a positive business case can provide the economic justification for investing in reuse, we also need ways to assess the economic benefits due to reuse. We need a realistic method of estimating the value of what we have done. Chapter 5, "Measuring Reuse and Reuse Benefits," examined representative reuse economic models. Several of these models use a simple cost–benefit analysis to determine whether or not to invest; if the benefits outweigh the costs, then the organization should invest in reuse. However, determining all the costs and benefits can lead to much tedious or impossible data collection. To simplify this task, Chapter 3, "The Relative Costs of Developing with and for Reuse," introduced two new terms:

1. The *Relative Cost of Reuse (RCR)*, for the cost of reusing software relative to writing new code, and

2. The *Relative Cost of Writing for Reuse (RCWR)*, for the cost of writing reusable software relative to writing software for one-time use.

The most accurate use of *RCR* and *RCWR* comes when an organization uses its own values for these terms. However, since most organizations do not have historical information available to derive their own values, we provided extensive experience reports to suggest default values. From these we stated the following two key observations:

> **Reusing software takes 20% of the effort of new development, so:**
>   **RCR = 0.2.**

> **Writing software for reuse takes 50% extra effort, so:**
>   **RCWR = 1.5.**

This book uses default values of $RCR = 0.2$ and $RCWR = 1.5$. Organizations can use these values to estimate the costs they avoid by reusing software and the costs required to build reusable software. Chapter 6, "Implementing a Metrics Program," gave a recommended "starter set" of reuse metrics based on RCR and RCWR. These basic metrics can provide the basic information needed by any reuse program:

- **Reuse%** for measuring reuse level,
- **Reuse Cost Avoidance (RCA)** for estimating the benefits an organization receives from reusing software, and
- **Project ROI** for estimating the benefits of reuse to a group of organizations working on a project.

In Chapter 7, "Measuring Software Reusability," we started with the key observation that no one can agree on an answer to the question:

> **What makes software reusable?**

Although many researchers have made significant attempts at an answer, the question remains open. To help classify the many approaches to measuring reusability, "A Taxonomy of Reusability Metrics" on page 110 divided the many methods into those that use (1) primarily empirical or (2) primarily qualitative criteria. The approaches we examined uncovered many different and interesting attributes that contribute to the reusability of software. However, they also discovered many of the same attributes. We grouped these attributes together in "A Common Model for Reusability" on page 130. In addition to these common attributes, we concluded that the usefulness of a component often depends on factors external to the component. For example, we cannot reuse a component unless it will work within the software architecture or the DSSA where we want to use it. From this we made the following key observation:

> **Software reusability depends on attributes from the environment as well as individual components.**

Chapter 8, "Metrics for Reuse Libraries," contained measures to assess and improve the effectiveness of an organization's Software Reuse Library (RSL):

1. *The number of accesses to the RSL*
2. *The number of accesses per component*
3. *Source Instructions Reused by Others (SIRBO)*
4. *RSL ROI*
5. *Library Efficiency*

We showed how to interpret these metrics and, most importantly, how to use the SIRBO and RSL ROI to demonstrate the value of the RSL to an organization. Finally, this chapter explained why, despite its popularity, the *total number of components in the RSL* does not make a good RSL metric because it does not reflect the usefulness of the components in the RSL.

Chapter 9, "Measuring Reuse Across the Life Cycle," presented a basic reuse level metric, *Life Cycle Reuse%*, for assessing the overall impact of reuse that occurs in all phases of the software development life cycle. Because the coding phase takes only one portion of this life cycle, focusing on code reuse gives only a limited view of the overall effect of reuse. However, we currently do not have the ability to quantify work products other than code in all life-cycle phases. Because of this, and the abundance of evidence to show that LOC faithfully represent the total amount of effort across the software life cycle, we made a key observation:

> **Lines of Code work as an overall indicator of reuse.**

The reuse levels we calculate using lines of code give us a good approximation of the total amount of life cycle reuse. We expect to continue to use this key observation until we develop dependable and repeatable methods of measuring our work products in all life-cycle phases.

Measuring reuse and quantifying its benefits take the guesswork out of a reuse program and demonstrate the value of an organization's investment. Nothing convinces people faster than concise, honest assumptions and a simple, understandable model that yields surprisingly favorable results. This book contains the basic metrics upon which to build a successful reuse program.

❖ WHERE DO WE GO FROM HERE?

This book brought together a number of representative works in the field of reuse metric and economic models. The list of problems we have solutions for includes these:

1. Defining what to count as reuse,
2. Assessing the level of reuse in an application or organization, and
3. Estimating the benefits of reuse in terms of cost avoidance or ROI.

However, many unresolved issues remain:

1. Measuring reuse in all phases of the software life-cycle,
2. Applying our reuse metric and economic models,
3. Validating our models,
4. Incorporating *software architecture* and *domain* issues into our view of software reusability, and
5. Evolving our view of reuse as our software development practices mature.

We conclude this book with a final look at these unresolved issues. They will make interesting areas for future work.

1. **Measuring non-code reuse.** As discussed in Chapter 9, "Measuring Reuse Across the Life Cycle," until we understand the issues behind reuse in other

phases of the life-cycle, such as requirements, design, information development, and test cases, we will use LOC as an overall indicator of reuse. LOC allows us to use readily available tools and objective evidence to quantify the amount of reuse on an application. However, we need more work on identifying and validating units for use across the software life cycle. Once this happens we will have a much better perspective on the total benefits of reuse.

2. **Applying reuse metric and economic models.** After the development and publication of a metric model, we rarely see follow-up reports that detail reuse experiences using the models. It seems that few organizations actually use the models they have developed; to properly assess progress and accomplishments in the field of reuse, we need to consistently report metrics first within our organizations and then as a profession.

We certainly do not need more reuse metric models. Developing an equation that accounts for the costs and benefits of reuse does not require much work; this book provided an overview of some of the major models already in existence. The hard part is supplying the data to put into the equations. How do you determine all the costs and all the benefits? This book made a significant contribution to reuse economics in that it took on the difficult issue of determining what data to use when calculating reuse levels and benefits. We now need more experience reports using a common counting model such as that presented in Chapter 3.

3. **Validating reuse metric and economic models.** Metrics yield values based on the equation in the metric and on the data that we put into the equation. This book emphasized the importance of the data we use in our models. Unfortunately, organizations that have data do not always publicize it for reasons of confidentiality. Furthermore, because practically no organization has the resources to complete a project two ways (once with reuse and once without), we have to rely on estimates and projections of reuse benefits. The field of reuse metrics needs experimental data and data based on comparable experiences in order to assess our models and to quantitatively research the factors leading to successful reuse [126].

Analytical research could help identify these factors by using population studies to see the effects on projects that do and do not practice reuse. This approach, developed in the social sciences, measures the statistical similarity of issues and give a probability that an outcome will occur. This eliminates the need to do a project twice to get a comparison. For reuse, we can describe the characteristics of projects using domain analysis and keep data on the actual results of these projects. Allowing for the degree of similarity between projects and given enough data points, we can develop a statistical correlation between reuse and results.

4. **Reusability metrics.** Researchers continue the search for a general reusability metric. However, we have seen from our examination of the reusability criteria in Chapter 7, "Measuring Software Reusability," that the critical factors are completely external to the software. A software architecture or domain framework largely determines the shape of the hole that the software must fill. The search for a general reusability metric will continue until we better understand the link between software and its environment.

5. **Our evolving view of reuse.** Finally, the state of the software development art changes constantly. The software engineering community will continue to introduce new tools, new methods, and new languages to make software development more productive and efficient. Some of these new innovations will come as the result of our work in reuse. They include techniques we have developed for raising abstraction levels, parameterizing software, and making generic interfaces. As our techniques progress, so do our perceptions of reuse. In the early 1960s, the introduction of macros allowed us to "reuse" common assembly code routines. We soon considered the repeated use of a macro as expected part of software development and stopped thinking of it as "reuse." Likewise, many of the techniques that we count as reuse today will fade into the fabric of software-development *business as usual.*

As reuse technology and processes mature, what we now call *reuse* will eventually cease to exist. Ruben Prieto-Diaz states that the ultimate success of software reuse will occur when it disappears from the forefront of our consciousness [117]. As with other engineering disciplines, this disappearance will not come by elimination but by integration into our business. As we integrate the activities that we now measure as reuse into our development cycle, we will have to modify our definition of "what to count."

❖

Appendix A:
Reuse
Metric Worksheets

DATA COLLECTION WORKSHEET

To gather data for reuse metrics we might request that each organization submit a worksheet similar to the one in Table 27. In cases where an organization has responsibility for developing one application, this worksheet will contain the reuse data for that application. In the first column of the worksheet, enter the name of each component used by the application (use one row per component). For each component (row), enter the number of LOC in that component in the appropriate column. Values for LOC normally come from a code analysis tool.

- If the component counts as a *reused* component, enter the LOC in the component in the second column.

- If the organization developed the component for reuse by others, enter the LOC in the third column.

- Finally, use the fourth column for the total lines of code in a component developed solely for use on the current project.

To calculate reuse levels (*Reuse%*) for the organization or application, we find the total LOC by summing the values in the three columns. We then calculate *Reuse%* by taking the sum of the RSI column and dividing by the total LOC.

TABLE 27 *Reuse Data Collection Worksheet for Application A*

Component	RSI (reused LOC)	LOC written for reuse	New or changed LOC
1. First Component	200	—	—
2. Second Component	—	100	—
3. Third Component	—	—	300
Application Totals	200	100	300

REUSE METRICS WORKSHEET

For large projects involving many organizations or applications, use a worksheet similar to Table 28. Fill out this worksheet using the data collection worksheet completed by each organization or application. Use one row for each organization or application, then sum each column and place the result in the last row. Use the totals in the last row to calculate metrics such as *Reuse%*, *Additional Development Costs (ADC)*, *Reuse Cost Avoidance (RCA)*, and *Project ROI* for the entire project.

TABLE 28 *Reuse Metrics Worksheet for Project P*

Organization/ application	RSI (reused LOC)	LOC written for reuse	New or changed LOC	Total LOC
1. Application A	200	100	300	600
2. Application B	150	50	200	400
Project Total	350	150	500	1000

REUSE METRICS SUMMARY SHEET

Table 29 summarizes the reuse data from the prior two worksheets. For each organization or application on the project, we have calculated the *Reuse%*, *Reuse Cost Avoided (RCA)*, *Additional Development Costs (ADC)*, and the resulting *Return on Investment (ROI)*. To complete this worksheet, we used the equations and default input values from "Case Study: Applying Reuse Metrics on a Project" on page 100.

Blank versions of each of these three worksheets are supplied in Tables 30–32.

TABLE 29 *Reuse Metrics Summary for Project P*

Organization/ application	Reuse%	RCA	ADC	ROI
1. Application A	33%	$18,000	$15,000	$3,000
2. Application B	37.5%	$13,500	$7,500	$6,000
Project Total	35%	$31,500	$22,500	$9,000

TABLE 30 *Reuse Data Collection Worksheet for Application* _____

Component	RSI (reused LOC)	LOC written for reuse	New or changed LOC
1.			
2.			
3.			
4.			
5.			
6.			
7.			
8.			
9.			
10.			
11.			
12.			
13.			
14.			
15.			
16.			
17.			
18.			
19.			
20.			
21.			
22.			
23.			
24.			
25.			
26.			
27.			
28.			
29.			
30.			
Application Totals			

TABLE 31 *Reuse Metrics Worksheet for Project* _____

Organization/application	RSI (reused LOC)	LOC written for reuse	New or changed LOC	Total LOC
1.				
2.				
3.				
4.				
5.				
6.				
7.				
8.				
9.				
10.				
11.				
12.				
13.				
14.				
15.				
16.				
17.				
18.				
19.				
20.				
21.				
22.				
23.				
24.				
25.				
26.				
27.				
28.				
29.				
30.				
Project Total				

TABLE 32 *Reuse Metrics Summary for Project* ————————————————————

Organization/application	*Reuse%*	*RCA*	*ADC*	*ROI*
1.				
2.				
3.				
4.				
5.				
6.				
7.				
8.				
9.				
10.				
11.				
12.				
13.				
14.				
15.				
16.				
17.				
18.				
19.				
20.				
21.				
22.				
23.				
24.				
25.				
26.				
27.				
28.				
29.				
30.				
Project Total				

Appendix B: Reuse Metric Calculator

Automating a set of reuse metrics and ROI models can greatly assist an organization in instituting the metrics. Providing tools to do the calculations makes using the metrics easy and more likely to be used. Fortunately, because of the proliferation of spreadsheets almost anyone can enter the equations onto a personal computer and experiment with input values to see the results. Some of the economic models discussed in this book have companion spreadsheets available on the Internet, such as the SPC model [31] and one based on the SPC model [122].

To this end we developed a simple spreadsheet tool that consists of two simple screens (plus on-line help). We present the tool here to encourage organizations to develop similar tools for their own reuse metrics. To use the spreadsheet, a user enters the input data and assumptions on the the first screen, as shown in Figure 15. If the user has actual data and wishes to override the default values for software development costs, etc., the user simply types over the defaults.

The input values represent an organization working on an application consisting of a total of 120K LOC; 100K LOC of new, added, or changed source lines and 20K LOC of reused components. In addition, the organization incurred an additional cost by developing 15K LOC (of the 100K LOC that they had to write) especially for reuse by others. The organization uses the default values of $RCR = 0.2$ and $RCWR = 1.5$. Finally, they obtained historical data for their organization showing a base cost of $100 per line of new code, an error rate of 1.5 errors per KLOC, and a cost of $10K to fix each reported error.

Note that two other organizations have committed to use portions of the code developed for reuse in this example. Group A will use 12K LOC of the code written for reuse; Group A has a new code development cost of $200/LOC, an RCR of 0.2, an error rate of 2 errors per KLOC, and a cost to fix an error of $10K. Group B will use all 15K LOC of the code written for reuse; they have a new code development cost of

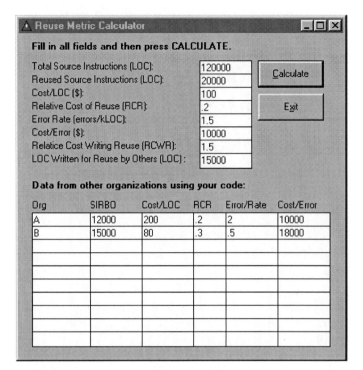

FIGURE 15 *Reuse Metric Calculator—Input Screen*

$80/LOC, an RCR of 0.3, an error rate of 0.5 errors per KLOC, and a cost to fix an error of $18K. Once we have entered this data and hit the enter key, the computer performs the calculations and displays the output screen shown in Figure 16.

The output screen reiterates some of the input values and shows all the calculated reuse metrics. First, the 20K LOC RSI represents a *Reuse%* of 16.67% for the organization. The 15K LOC they developed for reuse represents 15% of the 100K LOC developed for the application and cost an additional $0.75 million. However, organizations A and B benefit from this investment by using 27K LOC of the code; this increases our example organization's relative productivity as shown by *RVA* = 1.47. The direct benefits to this organization amount to $1.9 million in RCA.

The other organizations (Groups A and B) had a combined RCA of $3.135 million. Taking the total Reuse Cost Avoidance benefit of all three organizations and subtracting off the Additional Development Cost incurred to write the reusable software, the total cost avoided across the project comes to $4.285 million.

A reuse metric spreadsheet not only gives users an easy way to generate their reuse metrics, it also provides them with a nice tool for generating "what-if" scenarios using their own assumptions. Users quickly discover that the model shows impressive

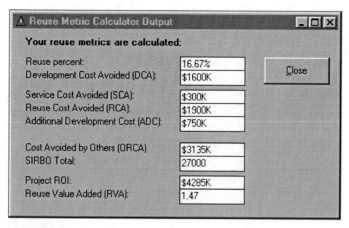

FIGURE 16 *Reuse Metric Calculator—Output Screen*

benefits from even very conservative assumptions. This can help "sell" the benefits of reuse to an organization!

❖

Appendix C: Reuse
Metric
Glossary

Abstract class

A class in an object-oriented program that acts as a template for other classes, usually at the root of a class hierarchy.

Application (software)

A software program of any size. See *Boundary problem*.

Asset (software)

Any reusable item in the software life-cycle: requirements, design documents, code, test cases, etc.

Base code

The product base consists of all code previously released in earlier versions of the product.

Black-box reuse

The reuse of unmodified software *components*.

Boundary problem

For a software component to be classified as "reused," it must come from another context: e.g., another *organization* or software *application*. The boundary problem leads to guidelines for making this determination.

Component (software)

A module, procedure, function, etc., of software intended for reuse, including all supporting documentation, integration instructions, test cases, and other information to help a potential reuser evaluate and employ the software. See *module*.

Consumer

A person or *organization* that reuses software.

Cost avoidance

The financial benefit resulting from not having to expend resources. By reusing software, an *organization* avoids a cost proportional to the cost of having to develop that software.

Cyclomatic complexity

A metric based on graph theory that reflects the total number of paths through a software *module*. See McCabe [94].

Deferred class

A class in an object-oriented program that does not contain implementations for all of its operations. This language mechanism allows the programmer to specify the need for operations but allows subclasses to provide their own implementations.

Domain

An application area which may contain many related application programs.

Domain analysis

The formal study of an application area, primarily to identify opportunities for reuse across application programs in that *domain*.

Domain engineering

The design and implementation of software and rules for its use within a specific *domain*. Domain engineering normally involves the development of reusable components designed specifically for use in the candidate domain. Selecting and defining these components normally takes place during *domain analysis*.

Domain-specific reuse

The reuse of components within an application *domain*. These components usually result from an intense study, or *domain analysis*, of the domain to identify the candidate reusable components, followed by building of the components via *domain engineering*.

Domain-Specific Software Architecture (DSSA)

A *software architecture* of a specific application *domain*. A DSSA normally contains reference requirements, a domain model, and tools with a well-defined process to support working with the requirements and domain model.

Estimate

A calculated value that approximates the actual value of some attribute. We define an estimate as the point where, to the best of our knowledge, we have an equal probability of having calculated a value greater than or less than the actual value of the attribute.

External reuse

Use of software from another *organization*. See *Boundary problem*.

Halstead complexity

A metric based on cognitive theory derived from the total numbers of operators and operands in a software *module*. See *McCabe Metrics* and the book by Halstead [57].

Horizontal reuse

Reuse of domain-independent *components*. See also *domain-specific reuse;* horizontal reuse generally takes place with low-level, simple components and therefore cannot lead to the higher reuse levels possible via *vertical reuse*.

Inheritance

An object-oriented language mechanism that allows the extension of a class into subclasses by specializing the existing class to allow subclasses to share common features.

Internal reuse

Use of software within an *organization*, a normal procedure in software development that does not count as "reuse." See *Boundary problem*.

Labor-Month (LM)

A unit of effort; the amount of work a person can do in one work month (about 22 days).

Leveraged code

The use of modified software in a new application; see *Reengineering*.

Life-Cycle Reuse%

The reuse level of a project measured by summing the actual levels of reuse during each phase of the software life-cycle and adjusting those levels for the amount of effort expended in that life-cycle phase.

Lines of Code (LOC)

(1) A logical line of code in a programming language source file, informally counted by the number of semicolons in the code and formally counted according to rules established by documents such as [101]. (2) An indicator of overall effort on a program.

Logical Source Statements (LSS)

The number of lines of code in a source file, excluding blank lines and comments; roughly equivalent to the number of semicolons in the file for programming languages that use semicolons as line terminators (e.g., Ada). See also *Non-blank, non-comment source statements*.

McCabe metrics

See *Cyclomatic complexity* and the original paper by McCabe [94].

Metric, software

A quantifiable attribute of software, either directly measured or computed from values directly measured from the software.

Module

The code that makes up a self-contained software subprogram, such as a procedure, function, method, subroutine, or macro; the key reuse ingredient in a *component*.

Non-Blank, Non-Comment Source Statements (NBNCSS)

The number of lines of code in a source file, excluding blank lines and comments. See also *Logical source statements*.

Opportunistic reuse

The reuse of modified software *components*. See *Reengineering*.

Organization (of people)

A programming team, department, or other autonomous group with software development responsibility. Many organizations may contribute to software development on a large project. With regard to measuring reuse, we expect persons within an organization to follow good software engineering techniques (e.g., structure software into functions, classes, and procedures, which the organization then invokes to perform a higher-level function). See *Boundary problem*.

Physical Source Statements (PSS)

The number of lines in a source file, including blank lines and comments.

Planned reuse

The reuse of unmodified software *components* as takes place in an organized, systematic reuse program.

Polymorphism

An object-oriented language mechanism that provides for the use of the same name for the same operation on several data types by allowing several implementations for a common interface.

Producer

A person or organization that writes software for reuse by others.

Productivity index

A metric that shows how an *organization* changes productivity through reuse relative to an organization that does not participate in reuse, which has a productivity index equal to 1.

Project

A large software development effort, typically made up of many *organizations.*

Reengineering

The use of existing software in a new *application,* usually after modifying the software. The technically correct term for *opportunistic reuse, white-box reuse, salvaging,* etc.

Relative Cost of Reuse (RCR)

The portion of the effort that it takes to reuse a *component* without modification versus writing it new.

Relative Cost of Writing for Reuse (RCWR)

The portion of the effort that it takes to write a reusable *component* versus writing it for one-time use only.

Return on Investment (ROI)

A long-term economic benefit. For reuse metrics, ROI analysis usually involves assessing the costs and benefits of a reuse program, to include factors for the time value of money.

Reusability

The attributes or characteristics of software that affect a developer's ability to reuse the software.

Reusable component

See *Component (software).*

Reusable Software Library (RSL)

(1) A collection of software *components* intended for *reuse.* (2) A tool that stores and manages reusable components.

Reuse

The incorporation into an *application* of unmodified software *components* obtained from other programs external to the *application.* These external sources typically include other applications, other *organizations,* and reuse libraries. For further discussion, see the IEEE definition [64].

Reuse level

The portion of a program coming from reused software, generally expressed as a percentage of the total source lines for the program.

Reuse leverage

An indicator of the "multiplier" effect of reuse, used as a *productivity index*.

Reuse maturity

A variation of the Software Engineering Institute (SEI) process Capability Maturity Model (CMM) used to describe how well an *organization* has developed and practices reuse.

Reuse ratio

An indicator of *reuse level*; the decimal equivalent of a percentage. Sometimes used to mean *reuse leverage*.

Reused Source Instruction (RSI)

Software that complies with the reuse definition in Chapter 4, "Defining Reuse from a Metrics Point of View."

Salvaging

Unplanned reuse; the reuse of modified software *components*. See *Reengineering*.

Source Instructions Reused by Others (SIRBO)

The total amount of software produced for reuse by an *organization* or in a *Reusable Software Library* that other organizations actually reuse.

Software

(1) Used to refer to code only. (2) All work products resulting from the software in addition to code: e.g., documentation, design documents, test cases.

Software architecture

The highest-level organization of a software system.

Systematic reuse

The reuse of unmodified software *components*. See *Black-box reuse*.

Unplanned reuse

The use of modified software *components*. See *Reengineering*.

Vertical reuse

Reuse of *components* within a *domain*. See also *Domain-specific reuse;* vertical reuse can lead to much higher reuse levels than *horizontal reuse*.

White-box reuse

The reuse of modified software *components*. See *Reengineering*.

❖

Appendix D:
Acronyms

Term	Meaning
3C	Concept, Content, Context
AAS	Advanced Automation System
ADC	Additional Development Cost
ADT	Abstract Data Type
API	Application Programming Interface
ARC	Army Reuse Center
ASDS	Advanced Simulation Development System
AT&T	American Telephone and Telegraph
BAU	Business as Usual
CASE	Computer Aided Software Engineering
CCTT	Close Combat Tactical Trainer
CMM	Capability Maturity Model
COCOMO	COnstructive COst MOdel
COTS	Commercial off-the-Shelf

Term	Meaning
CSC	Computer Sciences Corporation
DCA	Development Cost Avoidance
DoD	Department of Defense
DSRS	Defense Software Repository System
DSSA	Domain-Specific Software Architecture
FAA	Federal Aviation Administration
FP	Function Point
GAO	General Accounting Office
GOTS	Government off-the-Shelf
HLL	High-Level Language
HP	Hewlett-Packard
HPS	High-Productivity Systems
IBM	International Business Machines
IP	Internet Protocol
IEEE	Institute of Electrical and Electronics Engineers

Term	Meaning	Term	Meaning
KDSI	Thousand(s) of Delivered Source Instructions	RCA	Reuse Cost Avoidance
		RCR	Relative Cost of Reuse
KLOC	Thousand(s) of Lines of Code	RCWR	Relative Cost of Writing for Reuse
LM	Labor-Month (also Programmer-Month)	REBOOT	REuse By Object-Oriented Techniques
LOC	Line(s) of Code	ROI	Return on Investment
LSS	Logical Source Statements	RSL	Reusable Software Library
MHVPL	Mid-Hudson Valley Programming Laboratory	RVA	Reuse Value Added
		SCA	Service Cost Avoidance
MVS	Multiple Virtual Storage	SEI	Software Engineering Institute
NASA	National Aeronautics and Space Administration	SIRBO	Source Instructions Reused by Others
NATO	North Atlantic Treaty Organization	SPC	Software Productivity Consortium
NPV	Net Present Value	STARS	Software Technology for Adaptable, Reliable Systems
OO	Object-Oriented		
OS	Operating System	US	United States
PDL	Program Design Language	WWW	World-Wide-Web
		WYSIWYG	What-You-See-Is-What-You-Get
PSS	Physical Source Statements		

Appendix E:
Recommended
Reading

OVERVIEWS OF REUSE

GAO, "Software Reuse—Major Issues Need to Be Resolved Before Benefits Can Be Achieved," *United States General Accounting Office (GAO)*, GAO/IMTEC-93-16, January 1993.

Many papers, books, and manuscripts contain overviews of the major issues in the field of reuse. However, most of these overviews present reuse from a particular viewpoint. This reference contains the GAO report on the status of reuse efforts in the U.S. Federal Government. As a prelude to that report, it also contains an excellent unbiased overview of reuse that spans technical, organizational, and legal issues.

Krueger, Charles W., "Software Reuse," *Computing Surveys*, Vol. 24, No. 2, June 1992, pp. 131–183.

A thorough survey of the reuse state-of-the-art as of 1991–1992, including many timeless issues and discussions on reuse methods and issues. The survey discusses the reuse effects of high-level languages (HLLs), application generators, transformational systems, and software architectures.

Prieto-Diaz, Ruben, and Peter Freeman, "Classifying Software for Reusability," *IEEE Software*, Vol. 4, No. 1, January 1987, pp. 6–16.

The reference on software classification for reuse; this paper introduced the faceted classification method to the field. The paper covers a wide range of additional topics and issues, from encouraging white-box reuse, to finding candidates for reuse in existing software, to evaluating the easiest candidate components to modify and reuse. The paper discusses reusability, giving five criteria (metrics) for evaluating reusable components. A very important and perhaps the premier article in the field; a must read.

Tracz, Will, *Confessions of a Used Program Salesman.* Addison-Wesley, Reading, MA, 1995.

This book brings together the real difficulties of software reuse in a tongue-in-cheek, easy-to-read series of essays and "lessons learned." The book covers issues such as management concerns, the "not invented here" syndrome, and reuse processes. Highly recommended and enjoyable, the book makes an excellent and informative presentation for readers who both want to learn about reuse and who want to laugh a little over anecdotes that may reflect their own experiences.

DOMAIN ANALYSIS

Arango, Guillermo, "Domain Analysis Methods," in *Software Reusability,* Wilhem Shaefer, Ruben Prieto-Diaz, and Masao Matsumoto, eds. Ellis Horwood, Chichester, U.K., 1993.

This book chapter gives an overview of issues related to domain analysis, domain engineering, etc. It then surveys the leading domain analysis methods with the purpose of identifying the common themes and processes. The resulting "common domain analysis model" emphasizes the similarities among the leading methods. It makes an excellent reference for learning about domain analysis, as well as helping an organization select a method for its own use.

RELATIVE COSTS OF REUSE

Favaro, John, "What Price Reusability? A Case Study," *Ada Letters,* Vol. 11, No. 3, Spring 1991, pp. 115–124.

This paper starts by describing reuse-in-the-small versus reuse-in-the-large; it classifies reuse-in-the-large as something similar to the integration of commercial, off-the-shelf products, such as the use of spreadsheets or databases. The paper further distinguishes itself by raising, for perhaps the first time, the issue of "what to count" and how to differentiate between "use" and "reuse." Most importantly, this paper reports reliable values for the Relative Cost of Reuse (RCR) and the Relative Cost of Writing for Reuse (RCWR).

REUSE METRIC MODELS

DISA/JIEO/CIM, "Software Reuse Metrics Plan," *Defense Information Systems Agency, Joint Interoperability Engineering Organization, Center for Information Management,* Version 4.1, 4 August 1993.

The official DISA/CIM reuse metrics for use throughout the United States Department of Defense. Based on the metrics developed for IBM [104], the DISA metrics distinguish between adaptive (white-box) and verbatim (black-box) reuse and report them separately. The cost avoidance metric does not include maintenance savings. A thorough document, complete with worksheets and samples, and an excellent attempt to achieve a standardized method for reporting software reuse.

Gaffney, John E., Jr., and Thomas Durek, "Software Reuse—Key to Enhanced Productivity; Some Quantitative Models," *Software Productivity Consortium, SPC-TR-88-015,* April 1988.

The reuse metrics model by John Gaffney *et al.* Widely published and distributed, this reference represents just one of a series of publications, including the more recent [32]. The model emphasizes the payoffs of reuse by studying the relationship between the cost to produce a reusable component and the number of expected reuses that an organization can expect to receive of that component.

Poulin, Jeffrey S., Debera Hancock, and Joseph M. Caruso, "The Business Case for Software Reuse," *IBM Systems Journal,* Vol. 32, No. 4, 1993, pp. 567–594.

Starting with an introduction to major issues in reuse metrics, this paper describes the business case for reuse using the reuse metric and ROI model adopted by IBM and others. Using cost/benefit and time value ROI based on the metrics, the paper presents the three IBM reuse metrics as well as the project-level and corporate-level ROI models. A good mixture of overview, rationale, and technical detail on reuse metrics in general and the IBM metrics in particular.

EXPERIENCE REPORTS

Lim, Wayne C., "Effects of Reuse on Quality, Productivity, and Economics," *IEEE Software,* Vol. 11, No. 5, September 1994, pp. 23–30.

An excellent industry experience paper based on data gathered at Hewlett-Packard. The data reflects efforts and techniques developed over many years by the reuse team at HP and serves as a good example of the potential and payoff of reuse, especially within domain-specific product lines. This paper appears in a special issue of *IEEE Software* on software reuse that also contains several other noteworthy papers.

Margano, Johan, and Thomas E. Rhoads, "Software Reuse Economics: Cost Benefit Analysis on a Large Scale Ada Project," *Proceedings of the International Conference on Software Engineering,* Melbourne, Australia, 11–15 May 1992, pp. 338–348.

This report details reuse results on the extremely large project to update the Federal Aviation Administration Advance Air Traffic Control System (FAA/AAS) at IBM, Rockville, Maryland. The paper reports on organization and results, showing excellent reuse levels using several of the reuse models presented in this book.

Selby, Richard W., "Quantitative Studies of Software Reuse," in *Software Reusability*, Volume 2, Ted J. Biggerstaff and Alan J. Perlis (eds.). Addison-Wesley, Reading, MA, 1989.

This book chapter provides a cogent, thorough, statistical study of the reusability characteristics of software, using data from a NASA software production environment doing ground support software for unmanned spacecraft in FORTRAN. The study provides empirical evidence (most at the 0.05 level of confidence) that modules reused without modification tend to have smaller size, good documentation, simple interfaces, and little input–output (via parameters, coupling with other modules, and human interaction). Perhaps the most well-done and respected analysis of the attributes of software reusability.

OBJECT-ORIENTED REUSE

Cockburn, Alistair, "The Impact of Object-Orientation on Application Development," *IBM Systems Journal,* Vol. 32, No. 3, 1993, pp. 420–444.

An excellent description of a software development using object-oriented techniques. As part of that discussion, the paper also gives perhaps one of the most comprehensive and responsible descriptions of software reuse in the object-oriented paradigm. Cockburn explains the advantages and disadvantages of OO language features in terms of how their use can propagate "clean" and "messy" changes throughout an OO program.

SOFTWARE METRICS

Fenton, Norman E., "Software Measurement: A Necessary Scientific Basis," *IEEE Transactions on Software Engineering,* Vol. SE-20, No. 3, March 1994, pp. 199–206.

This very accessible article is an excellent overview of software metric theory and its application. Fenton notes that most techniques for software measurement do not adhere to the science of measurement, and that an analyst can avoid this trap by observing some very simple, but fundamental, principles of measurement. The paper applies measurement theory to highlight both weaknesses and strengths of applied software metrics, including work on metrics validation. Fenton then demonstrates the concepts by examining the search for a general software complexity measure. See Fenton's book for details [41].

Roche, John, and Mike Jackson, "Software Measurement Methods: Recipes for Success?" *Information and Software Technology,* Vol. 36, No. 3, March 1994, pp. 173–189.

Roche and Jackson give a very good overview and comparison of seven software measurement methods, including the Factor-Criteria Metric (McCall), Quality Function Deployment (QFD) (Kogure and Akao), Constructive Quality Model (COQUAMO) from REBOOT, Goal-Question-Metric (GQM) (Basili), the 10 Step Metric Programme (Grady and Caswell at Hewlett-Packard), Application of Measurement in Industry (AMI), and Process Maturity Based Approach (Pfleeger). The article highlights the deficiencies of most metrics methods and defines a basic measurement process of Collection, Analysis, Interpretation, then (most often left out) Validation. A very good reference for readers interested in software metric methods.

References

1. Adamczyk, Jim, and Tom Modauer, "Trading Off: Inheritance vs. Reuse," *Object Magazine,* Vol. 5, No. 5, September 1995, pp. 56–59.

2. Anthes, Gary H., "Software Reuse Plans Bring Paybacks," *Computerworld,* Vol. 27, No. 49, pp. 73, 76.

3. Arango, Guillermo, "Domain Analysis Methods," in *Software Reusability.* Wilhem Shaefer, Ruben Prieto-Diaz, and Masao Matsumoto, eds. Ellis Horwood, Chichester, U.K., 1993.

4. Bailey, John W., and Victor Basili, "Software Reclamation: Improving Post-development Reusability," *8th Annual National Conference on Ada Technology,* 1990.

5. Bailey, John W., and Victor R. Basili, "The Software Cycle Model for Reengineering and Reuse," *Proceedings TRI-Ada 91,* San Jose, CA, 21–25 October 1991, pp. 267–281.

6. Balda, David M., and David A. Gustafson, "Cost Estimation Models for the Reuse and Prototype Software Development Lifecycles," *ACM SIGSOFT Software Engineering Notes,* Vol. 15, No. 3, July 1990, pp. 42–50.

7. Banker, Rajiv D., Robert J. Kauffman, and Dani Zweig, "Repository Evaluation of Software Reuse," *IEEE Transactions on Software Engineering,* Vol. 19, No. 4, April 1993, pp. 379–389.

8. Banker, Rajiv D., Robert J. Kauffman, Charles Wright, and Dani Zweig, "Automating Output Size and Reuse Metrics in a Repository-Based Computer-Aided Software Engineering (CASE) Environment," *IEEE Transactions on Software Engineering,* Vol. SE-20, No. 3, March 1994, pp. 169–187.

9. Bardo, Tim, Dave Elliot, Tony Krysak, Mike Morgan, Rebecca Shuey, and Will Tracz, "CORE: A Product Line Success Story," *Crosstalk: The Journal of Defense Software Engineering,* Vol. 9, No. 3, March 1996, pp. 24–28.

10. Barnes, B. H., and T. B. Bollinger, "Making Reuse Cost Effective," *IEEE Software*, Vol. 8, No. 1, January 1991, pp. 13–24.

11. Basili, Victor R., H. Dieter Rombach, John Bailey, and Alex Delis, "Ada Reusability Analysis and Measurement," *Empirical Foundations of Information and Software Science V*, Atlanta, GA, 19–21 October 1988, pp. 355–368.

12. Bassett, Paul G., "Frame-Based Software Engineering," *IEEE Software*, Vol. 4, No. 7, July 1987, pp. 9–16.

13. Bauer, Dorothea, "A Reusable Parts Center," *IBM Systems Journal*, Vol. 32, No. 4, 1993, pp. 620–624.

14. Binder, Robert V., "Introduction: Special Issue on Object-Oriented Software Testing," *Communications of the ACM*, Vol. 37, No. 9, September 1994, p. 29.

15. Boehm, Barry W., *Software Engineering Economics*. Prentice Hall, Englewood Cliffs, NJ, 1981.

16. Boetticher, G., K. Srinivas, and D. Eichmann, "A Neural Net-based Approach to Software Metrics," *Proceedings of the 5th International Conference on Software Engineering and Knowledge Engineering*, San Francisco, CA, 14–18 June 1993, pp. 271–274.

17. Boetticher, Gary, and David Eichmann, "A Neural Network Paradigm for Characterizing Reusable Software," *Proceedings of the 1st Australian Conference on Software Metrics*, 18–19 November 1993.

18. Bollinger, T. B., and S. L. Pfleeger, "Economics of Reuse: Issues and Alternatives," *Information Software Technology*, Vol. 32, No. 10, December 1990, pp. 643–652.

19. Booch, Grady, *Software Components with Ada: Structures, Tools, and Subsystems*. Benjamin Cummings, Menlo Park, CA, 1987.

20. Bourland, D. David, and Paul Dennithorne Johnston, eds., *To Be or Not: An E-Prime Anthology, International Society for General Semantics*, San Francisco, CA, 1991.

21. Brooks, Fred P., Jr., *The Mythical Man-Month*, Addison-Wesley, Reading, MA, 1975.

22. Caldiera, Gianluigi, and Victor R. Basili, "Identifying and Qualifying Reusable Software Components," *IEEE Computer*, Vol. 24, No. 2, February 1991, pp. 61–70.

23. Caldwell, Bruce, "Software Reuse Comes of Age," *InformationWEEK*, November 1994, p. 122.

24. Canfora, G., A. Cimitile, M. Munro, and M. Tortorella, "Experiments in Identifying Reusable Abstract Data Types in Program Code," *Proceedings IEEE Second Workshop on Program Comprehension*, Capri, Italy, 8–9 July 1993, pp. 36–45.

25. Chang, S. C., A. P. M. Groot, H. Oosting, J. C. van Vleit, and E. Willemsz, "A Reuse Experiment in the Social Security Sector," *Reusability Track of the 1994 ACM Symposium on Applied Computing (SAC '94)* Phoenix, Arizona, 6–8 March 1994, pp. 94–98.

26. Chen, Deng-Jyi, and P. J. Lee, "On the Study of Software Reuse Using Reusable C++ Components," *Journal of Systems Software*, Vol. 20, No. 1, Jan. 1993, pp. 19–36.

27. Chen, Yih Farn, Balachander Krishnamurthy, and Kiem Phong Vo, "An Objective Reuse Metric: Model and Methodology," *Proceedings of the 5th European Software Engineering Conference (ESEC '95)*, Sitges, Spain, 25–28 September 1995, pp. 109–123.

28. Chidamber, Shyam R., and Chris F. Kemerer, "Towards a Metrics Suite for Object Oriented Design," *Proc. OOPSLA 1991*, ACM Press, October 1991, pp. 197–211.

29. Cockburn, Alistair, "The Impact of Object-Orientation on Application Development," *IBM Systems Journal*, Vol. 32, No. 3, 1993, pp. 420–444.

30. Conte, S. D., H. E. Dunsmore, and V. Y. Shen. *Software Engineering Metrics and Models*. Benjamin Cummings, CA, 1986.

31. Cruickshank, Robert D., and John E. Gaffney, Jr., "The Economics of Software Reuse," *Software Productivity Consortium SPC-92119-CMC*, Version 01.00.00, September 1991.

32. Cruickshank, R., H. Felber, J. Gaffney, and R. Werling, "Software Measurement Guidebook," *Software Productivity Consortium SPC-91060-CMC*, Version 2.0, August 1994.

33. Davis, Ted, "The Reuse Capability Model," *Crosstalk: The Journal of Defense Software Engineering*, March, 1994, pp. 5–8.

34. DISA/JIEO/CIM, "Software Reuse Metrics Plan," *Defense Information Systems Agency, Joint Interoperability Engineering Organization, Center for Information Management*, Version 4.1, 4 August 1993.

35. Edwards, Stephan, "An Approach for Constructing Reusable Software Components in Ada," *Strategic Defense Organization Pub # Ada233 662*, Washington, D.C., September 1990.

36. Endres, Albert, "Lessons Learned in an Industrial Software Lab," *IEEE Software*, September 1993, pp. 58–61.

37. Esteva, Juan Carlos, "Automatic Identification of Reuseable Components," *Proceedings of the 7th International Workshop on Computer Aided Software Engineering*, Toronto, 10–14 July 1995, pp. 80–87.

38. Fafchamps, Danielle, "Organizational Factors and Reuse," *IEEE Software*, Vol. 11, No. 5, September 1994, pp. 31–41.

39. Favaro, John, "What Price Reusability? A Case Study," *Ada Letters*, Vol. 11, No. 3, Spring 1991, pp. 115–124.

40. Favaro, John, "A Comparison of Approaches to Reuse Investment Analysis," *Fourth International Conference on Software Reuse (ICSR '4)*, Orlando, FL, 23–26 April 1996, pp. 136–145.

41. Fenton, Norman E., *Software Metrics: A Rigourous Approach*. Chapman & Hall, London, 1991.

42. Fenton, Norman E., "Software Measurement: A Necessary Scientific Basis," *IEEE Transactions on Software Engineering*, Vol. SE-20, No. 3, March 1994, pp. 199–206.

43. Ferrentino, Andrew B., "Large-Scale Software Reuse with Templates," *Proceedings of the National Symposium on Improving the Software Process and Competitive Position via Reuse and Reengineering*, Bethesda, MD, 18–19 November 1991.

44. Frakes, William B., "Software Reuse: Is It Delivering? (Panel)," *Proceedings of the 13th International Conference on Software Engineering*, Austin, TX, 13–16 May 1991, pp. 52–59.

45. Frakes, William, and Carol Terry, "Reuse Level Metrics," *Third International Conference on Software Reuse (ICSR '3)*, Rio de Janeiro, Brazil, 1–4 November 1994, pp. 139–148.

46. Gaffney, John E., Jr., and Thomas Durek, "Software Reuse—Key to Enhanced Productivity: Some Quantitative Models," *Software Productivity Consortium, SPC-TR-88-015*, April 1988.

47. Gaffney, J. E., Jr., and T. A. Durek, "Software Reuse—Key to Enhanced Productivity: Some Quantitative Models," *Information and Software Technology*, Vol. 31, No. 5, June 1989, pp. 258–267.

48. Gaffney, J. E. and R. D. Cruickshank, "A General Economics Model of Software Reuse," *Proceedings of the International Conference on Software Engineering*, Melbourne, Australia, 11–15 May 1992, pp. 327–337.

49. Gamma, Erich, Richard Helm, Ralph Johnson, and John Vlissides, "Design Patterns: Elements of Reusable Object-Oriented Software," Addison-Wesley, Reading, MA, 1995.

50. GAO, "Software Reuse—Major Issues Need to Be Resolved Before Benefits Can Be Achieved," *United States General Accounting Office (GAO)*, GAO/IMTEC-93-16, January 1993.

51. Gartner Report, "Software Engineering Strategies," *Strategic Analysis Report*, Gartner Group, Inc., April 30, 1991.

52. Gibbs, W. Wayt, "Software's Chronic Crisis," *Scientific American*, September 1994, pp. 86–95.

53. Gottlieb, Robert G., and S. Douglas Neal, "The Advanced Simulation Development System (ASDS)," *Proceedings of the 1994 Summer Computer Simulation Conference*, San Diego, CA, 18–20 July 1994, pp. 125–130.

54. Grady, Robert B. *Practical Software Metrics for Project Management and Process Improvement*. Prentice Hall, Englewood Cliffs, NJ, 1992.

55. Griss, Martin, "Software Reuse: Objects and Frameworks Are Not Enough," *Object Magazine*, February 1995, pp. 77–79.

56. Griss, Martin, "Software Reuse: A Process of Getting Organized," *Object Magazine*, May 1995, pp. 76-78.

57. Halstead, Maurice H., *Elements of Software Science*. Elsevier North-Holland, NY, 1977.

58. Harris, Kim, "Using an Economic Model to Tune Reuse Strategies," *Proceedings of the 5th International Workshop on Software Reuse (WISR '5)*, Palo Alto, CA, 26–29 October 1992.

59. Henderson-Sellers, B., "The Economics of Reusing Library Classes," *Journal of Object-Oriented Programming*, Vol. 6, No. 4, July–August 1993, pp. 43–50.

60. Henry, Emmanuel, and Benoit Faller, "Large-Scale Industrial Reuse to Reduce Cost and Cycle Time," *IEEE Software*, Vol. 12, No. 5, September 1995, pp. 47–53.

61. Hislop, Gregory W., "Using Existing Software in a Software Reuse Initiative," *The Sixth Annual Workshop on Software Reuse (WISR '96)*, 2–4 November 1993, Owego, NY.

62. Hollingsworth, Joe, *Software Component Design-for-Reuse: A Language Independent Discipline Applied to Ada*. Ph.D. Thesis, Dept. of Computer and Information Science, The Ohio State University, Columbus, OH, 1992.

63. Hooper, James W., and Chester, Rowena O., *Software Reuse Guidelines and Methods*. Plenum Press, NY, 1991.

64. IEEE, "Standard for Software Productivity Metrics," *IEEE Standard #1045-1992*, IEEE Computer Society Press, NY, 1992.

65. Incorvaia, Angelo J., and Alan M. Davis, "Case Studies in Software Reuse," *Proceedings of the Fourteenth Annual International Computer Software and Applications Conference*, Chicago, IL, 31 October–2 November 1990, pp. 301–306.

66. International Function Point Users Group (IFPUG), *Function Point Counting Practices Manual*, Release 4.0, January 1994, pp. 4-1 to 4-4.

67. Isoda, Sadahiro, "Experience Report on Software Reuse Project: Its Structure, Activities, and Statistical Results," *Proceedings of the International Conference on Software Engineering*, Melbourne, Australia, 11–15 May 1992, pp. 320–326.

68.   Johnson, S. C., "Yacc: Yet Another Compiler Compiler in the UNIX Programmer's Manual—Supplementary Documents, 7th ed.," *AT&T Bell Laboratories*, Indianapolis, IN, 1979.

69.   Jones, Capers, *Applied Software Measurement: Assuring Productivity and Quality.* McGraw-Hill, Inc., New York, NY, 1991.

70.   Jones, Capers, "Economics of Software Reuse," *IEEE Computer*, Vol. 27, No. 7, July 1994, pp. 106–107.

71.   Jones, Capers, "Backfiring: Converting Lines of Code to Function Points," *IEEE Computer*, Vol. 28, No. 11, November 1995, pp. 87–88.

72.   Kain, J. Bradford, "Measuring the ROI of Reuse," *Object Magazine*, Vol. 4, No. 3, June 1994, pp. 48–54.

73.   Karlsson, Even-Andre, Guttorm Sindre, and Tor Stalhane, "Techniques for Making More Reusable Components," *REBOOT Technical Report #41*, 7 June 1992.

74.   Karlsson, Even-Andre (ed.), *Software Reuse: A Holistic Approach.* Wiley, New York, NY, 1995.

75.   Kennedy, Brian M., "Design for Object-Oriented Reuse in the OATH Library," *Journal of Object-Oriented Programming (JOOP)*, July/August, 1992, pp. 51–57.

76.   Khairuddin, Hashim, and Elizabeth Key, "A Software Reusability Attributes Model," *International Journal of Computer Applied Technology*, Vol. 8, No. 1–2, 1995, pp. 69–77.

77.   Kitchenham, Barbara, and Kari Kansala, "Inter-item Correlations among Function Points," *Proceedings of the IEEE Computer Society International Software Metrics Symposium*, Baltimore, MD, 21–22 May 1993, pp. 11–15.

78.   Kolton, Philip, and Anita Hudson, "A Reuse Maturity Model," *Position Paper at the Annual Workshop on Software Reuse*, Center for Innovative Technology, Herndon, VA, 18–22 November 1991.

79.   Krueger, Charles W., "Software Reuse," *Computing Surveys*, Vol. 24, No. 2, June 1992, pp. 131–183.

80.   Krutz, W. K., K. Allen, and D. P. Olivier, "The Costs Related to Making Software Reusable," *Proceedings of TRI-Ada '91*, San Jose, CA, 21–25 October 1991, pp. 437–443.

81.   Lanergan, Robert G., and Brian A. Poynton, "Reusable Code—The Application Development Technique of the Future," *Proceedings of the Joint SHARE/ GUIDE/IBM Application Development Symposium*, October 1979, pp. 127–136.

82.   Lenz, Manfred, Hans Albrecht Schmid, and Peter F. Wolf, "Software Reuse through Building Blocks," *IEEE Software*, Vol. 4, No. 7, July 1987, pp. 34–42.

83. Lesk, M. E., and E. Schmidt, "Lex: A Lexical Analyzer Generator in the UNIX Programmer's Manual—Supplementary Documents, 7th ed.," *AT&T Bell Laboratories*, Indianapolis, IN, 1979.

84. Lim, Wayne C., "Effects of Reuse on Quality, Productivity, and Economics," *IEEE Software*, Vol. 11, No. 5, September 1994, pp. 23–30.

85. Lim, Wayne C., "Reuse Economics: A Comparison of Seventeen Models and Directions for Future Research," *Fourth International Conference on Software Reuse (ICSR)*, Orlando, FL, 23–26 April 1996, pp. 41–50.

86. Linn, Marcia C., and Michael J. Clancy, "The Case for Case Studies of Programming Problems," *Communications of the ACM*, Vol. 35, No. 3, March 1992, p. 121.

87. Malan, Ruth, and Kevin Wentzel, "Economics of Software Reuse Revisited," *Hewlett-Packard Technical Report HPL-93-31*, April 1993.

88. Margano, Johan, and Lynn Lindsey, "Software Reuse in the Air Traffic Control Advanced Automation System," *Joint Symposia and Workshops: Improving the Software Process and Competitive Position*, 29 April–3 May 1991, Alexandria, VA.

89. Margano, Johan, and Thomas E. Rhoads, "Software Reuse Economics: Cost Benefit Analysis on a Large Scale Ada Project," *Proceedings of the International Conference on Software Engineering*, Melbourne, Australia, 11–15 May 1992, pp. 338–348.

90. Mastaglio, Thomas W., and Robert Callahan, "A Large-Scale Complex Virtual Environment for Team Training," *IEEE Computer*, Vol. 28, No. 7, July 1995, pp. 49–56.

91. Matsumoto, Masao J., "Quantitative Evaluations of Software Quality Built in with Domain-Specific Disciplines," *Proceedings the 5th European Software Engineering Conference (ESEC '95)*, Sitges, Spain, 25–28 September 1995, pp. 438–456.

92. Matsumoto, Yoshihiro, "Some Experience in Promoting Reusable Software Presentation in Higher Abstraction Levels," *IEEE Transactions on Software Engineering*, Vol. 10, No. 5, September 1984, pp. 502–513.

93. Mayobre, Guillermo, "Using Code Reusability Analysis to Identify Reusable Components from the Software Related to an Application Domain," *Fourth Annual Workshop on Software Reuse (WISR '4)*, Reston, VA, 18–22 November 1991.

94. McCabe, T. J., "A Complexity Measure," *IEEE Transactions on Software Engineering*, SE-2, 1976, pp. 308–320.

95. Moller, Karl-Heinrich, and Daniel J. Paulish, "An Empirical Investigation of Software Fault Distribution," *Proceedings of the IEEE Computer Society International Software Metrics Symposium*, Baltimore, MD, 21–22 May 1993, pp. 82–90.

96. Musser, David R., and Alexander A. Stepanov, *The Ada Generic Library.* Springer-Verlag, NY, 1989.

97. NATO, "Standard for the Development of Reusable Software Components," *NATO Communications and Information Systems Agency,* 18 August 1991.

98. NATO, "Standard for Management of a Reusable Software Component Library," *NATO Communications and Information Systems Agency,* 18 August 1991.

99. Natori, Mari, Akira Kagaya, and Shinichi Honiden, "Reuse of Design Processes Based on Domain Analysis," *Fourth International Conference on Software Reuse (ICSR '4),* Orlando, FL, 23–26 April 1996, pp. 31–40.

100. Pant, Y., B. Henderson Sellers, and J. M. Verner, "Generalization of Object-Oriented Components for Reuse: Measurements of Effort and Size Change," *Journal of Object Oriented Programming,* Vol. 9, No. 2, May 1996, pp. 19–31, 41.

101. Park, Robert E., "Software Size Measurement: A Framework for Counting Source Statements," *Software Engineering Institute Technical Report,* CMU/SEI-92-TR-20, September 1992.

102. Pennell, James P., "An Assessment of Software Portability and Reusability for the WAM Program," *Institute for Defense Analysis,* Alexandria, VA, October 1990.

103. Piper, Joanne C., and Wanda L. Barner, "The RAPID Center Reusable Components (RSCs) Certification Process," *U.S. Army Information Systems Software Development Center—Washington,* Ft. Belvoir, VA.

104. Poulin, Jeffrey S., and Joseph M. Caruso, "Determining the Value of a Corporate Reuse Program," *Proceedings of the IEEE Computer Society International Software Metrics Symposium,* Baltimore, MD, 21–22 May 1993, pp. 16–27.

105. Poulin, Jeffrey S., "Issues in the Development and Application of Reuse Metrics in a Corporate Environment," *Fifth International Conference on Software Engineering and Knowledge Engineering,* San Francisco, CA, 16–18 June 1993, pp. 258–262.

106. Poulin, Jeffrey S., and Kathryn P. Yglesias, "Experiences with a Faceted Classification Scheme in a Large Reusable Software Library (RSL)," *Seventeenth Annual International Computer Software and Applications Conference (COMPSAC '17),* Phoenix, AZ, 3–5 November 1993, pp. 90–99.

107. Poulin, Jeffrey S., "A Method for Assessing Cross Life-Cycle Reuse," *Proceedings of the 6th International Workshop on Software Reuse (WISR '6),* Owego, NY, 2–4 November 1993.

108. Poulin, Jeffrey S., Debera Hancock, and Joseph M. Caruso, "The Business Case for Software Reuse," *IBM Systems Journal,* Vol. 32, No. 4, 1993, pp. 567–594.

109. Poulin, Jeffrey S., and Keith W. Werkman, "Software Reuse Libraries with Mosaic," *2nd International World Wide Web Conference: Mosaic and the Web*, Chicago, IL, 17–20 October 1994. URL: *http://www.ncsa.uiuc.edu/SDG/IT94/Proceedings/DDay/werkman/www94.html*.

110. Poulin, Jeffrey S., "Measuring Software Reusability," *Third International Conference on Software Reuse (ICSR '3)*, Rio de Janeiro, Brazil, 1–4 November 1994, pp. 126–138.

111. Poulin, Jeffrey S., "Measuring the Level of Reuse in Object-Oriented Development," *Proceedings of the 7th International Workshop on Software Reuse (WISR '7)*, St. Charles, IL, 28–30 August 1995.

112. Poulin, Jeffrey S., "Software Reuse on the Army SBIS Program," *Crosstalk: The Journal of Defense Software Engineering*, July 1995, pp. 19–24.

113. Poulin, Jeffrey S., "Populating Software Repositories: Incentives and Domain-Specific Software," *Journal of Systems and Software*, Vol. 30, No. 3, September 1995, pp. 187–199.

114. Pressman, R.S., *Software Engineering: A Practitioner's Approach*. McGraw-Hill, NY, 1992.

115. Prieto-Diaz, Ruben, and Peter Freeman, "Classifying Software for Reusability," *IEEE Software*, Vol. 4, No. 1, January 1987, pp. 6–16.

116. Prieto-Diaz, Ruben, "Implementing Faceted Classification for Software Reuse," *Communications of the ACM*, Vol. 34, No. 5, May 1991, pp. 88–97.

117. Prieto-Diaz, Ruben, "The Disappearance of Software Reuse," *Proceedings of the 3rd International Conference on Software Reuse (ICSR '3)*, Rio de Janeiro, Brazil, 1–4 November 1994, p. 225.

118. Rajlich, Vaclav, and Joao Silva, "A Case Study of Software Reuse in Vertical Domain," *Proceedings of the 4th Systems Reengineering Technology Workshop*, Monterey, CA, 8–10 February 1994, pp. 67–76.

119. Rajlich, Vaclav, and Joao H. Silva, "Evolution and Reuse of Orthogonal Architecture," *IEEE Transactions on Software Engineering*, Vol. 22, No. 2, February 1996, pp. 153–157.

120. Ramesh, M., and H. Raghav Rao, "Software Reuse: Issues and an Example," *Decision Support Systems*, Vol. 12, No. 1, August 1994, pp. 57–77.

121. RAPID, "RAPID Center Standards for Reusable Software," *U.S. Army Information Systems Engineering Command*, 3451-4-012/ 6.4, October 1990.

122. Raymond, George E., and David M. Hollis, "Software Reuse Economics Model," *Proceedings of WADAS '91: 7th Washington Ada Symposium Summer SIGAda Meeting*, McLean, VA, 17–21 June 1991, pp. 141–155.

123. Reifer, Donald J., "Reuse Metrics and Measurement—A Framework," *NASA/Goddard Fifteenth Annual Software Engineering Workshop*, 28 November 1990.

124. Reifer, Donald, "SOFTCOST-Ada: User Experiences and Lessons Learned at the Age of Three," *Proceedings of TRI-Ada '90*, Baltimore, MD, 3–7 December 1990, pp. 472–482.

125. Ribot, Danielle, Blandine Bongard, and Claude Villerman, "Development Lifecycle WITH Reuse," *Reusability Track of the 1994 ACM Symposium on Applied Computing (SAC '94)*, Phoenix, AZ, 6–8 March 1994, pp. 70–76.

126. Roche, John, and Mike Jackson, "Software Measurement Methods: Recipes for Success?" *Information and Software Technology*, Vol. 36, No. 3, March 1994, pp. 173–189.

127. Schach, Stephen R., "The Economic Impact of Software Reuse on Maintenance," *Journal of Software Maintenance, Research, and Practice*, Vol. 6, No. 4, July–August 1994, pp. 185–196.

128. Schach, Stephen R., and Xuefeng Yang, "Metrics for Targeting Candidates for Reuse: An Experimental Approach," *Proceedings of the ACM Symposium on Applied Computing (SAC '95)*, 1995, pp. 379–383.

129. Scheffe, H. *The Analysis of Variance*. John Wiley & Sons, New York, NY, 1995.

130. Schroath, Leonard T., "Configuration Management for Software Tests," *Hewlett-Packard Journal*, Vol. 44, No. 3, June 1993, pp. 53–59.

131. Selby, Richard W., "Quantitative Studies of Software Reuse," in *Software Reusability*, Volume 2, Ted J. Biggerstaff and Alan J. Perlis, eds. Addison-Wesley, Reading, MA, 1989.

132. Sommerville, I., L. Masera, and C. Demaria, "Practical Guidelines for Ada Reuse in an Industrial Environment," *Proceedings of the Second Symposium on Software Quality Techniques and Acquisition Criteria*, Florence, Italy, 29–31 May 1995, pp. 138–147. URL: *http://www.comp.lancs.ac.uk/computing/research/cseg/projects/APPRAISAL/*.

133. Stalhane, Tor, "Development of a Model for Reusability Assessment," *Proceedings of the Second Symposium on Software Quality Techniques and Acquisition Criteria*, Florence, Italy, 29–31 May 1995, pp. 111–123.

134. STARS, "Repository Guidelines for the Software Technology for Adaptable, Reliable Systems (STARS) Program," CDRL Sequence Number 0460, 15 March 1989.

135. Stevens, Barry, "Results from the Navy's RNTDS Architecture," *Sixth Annual Software Technology Conference*, Salt Lake City, UT, 10–15 April 1994.

136. Tausworthe, R. C, "Information Models of Software Productivity: Limits on Productivity Growth," *Journal of System Software*, Vol. 19, No. 2, October 1992, pp. 185–201.

137. Taylor, David, "The Use and Abuse of Reuse," *Object Magazine*, Vol. 6, No. 2, April 1996, pp. 16–18.

138. Thomas, W. M., A. Delis, and V. R. Basili, "An Evaluation of Ada Source Code Reuse," *Proceedings of 11th Ada Europe International Conference*, Zandvoort, Netherlands, 1–5 June 1992, pp. 80–91.

139. Torres, William R., and Mansur H. Samadzadeh, "Software Reuse and Information Theory Based Metrics," *Proc. 1991 Symposium on Applied Computing (SAC '91)*, Kansas City, MO, 3–5 April 1991, pp. 437–446.

140. Tracz, Will, "Software Reuse Myths," *ACM SIGSOFT Software Engineering Notes*, Vol. 13, No. 1, Jan. 1988, pp. 17–21.

141. Tracz, Will, "Software Reuse Maxims," *ACM SIGSOFT Software Engineering Notes*, Vol. 13, No. 4, October 1988, pp. 28–31.

142. Tracz, Will, "A Conceptual Model for Megaprogramming," *ACM SIGSOFT Software Engineering Notes*, Vol. 16, No. 3, July 1991, pp. 36–45.

143. Tracz, Will, Lou Coglianese, and Patrick Young, "A Domain-Specific Software Architecture Engineering Process Outline," *ACM SIGSOFT Software Engineering Notes*, Vol. 18, No. 2, April 1993, pp. 40–49.

144. Tracz, Will, *Confessions of a Used Program Salesman*. Addison-Wesley, Reading, MA, 1995.

145. UNIX News, "Code Re-use Is the Object," *UNIX News*, May 1995, p. 48.

146. Weyuker, E. J., "Evaluating Software Complexity Measures," *IEEE Transactions on Software Engineering*, Vol. 14, No. 9, September 1988, pp. 1357–1365.

147. Woodfield, Scott N., David W. Embley, and Del T. Scott, "Can Programmers Reuse Software?" *IEEE Software*, Vol. 4, No. 7, July 1987, pp. 168–175.

148. Yglesias, Kathryn P., "Limitations of Certification Standards in Achieving Successful Parts Retrieval," *Proceedings of the 5th International Workshop on Software Reuse (WISR '5)*, Palo Alto, CA, 26–29 October 1992.

149. Zhuo, Fang, Bruce Lowther, Paul Oman, and Jack Hagemeister, "Constructing and Testing Software Maintainability Assessment Models," *Proceedings of the IEEE Computer Society International Software Metrics Symposium*, Baltimore, MD, 21–22 May 1993, pp. 61–70.

150. Zuse, H., "Criteria for Program Comprehension Derived from Software Complexity Metrics," *Proceedings IEEE Second Workshop on Program Comprehension*, Capri, Italy, 8–9 July 1993, pp. 8–16.

Index

A

Ada^R, 4, 6, 22, 28–29, 128–29
Adapted reused code, 83
Additional Development Cost (ADC), 81, 99
Application (software), 2
Application developers, 94
Application generators, measuring, 44–45
Application-specific software, 6
AT&T, 23, 56

B

Backfiring, 40
Balda, David M., 70–73, 86–87, 88
Banker, Rajiv D., 62–63
Bardo, Tim, 24, 28
Barnes, B. H., 73–74, 87, 89
Basili, Victor R., 119–20
BB/LX language, 28
Black-box versus white-box reuse, 2–3
Boetticher, Gary, 121
Bollinger, T. B., 73–74, 87, 89
Boundary problem
    ignoring, problems with, 35–36
    small versus large projects and, 36–39
software sharing within versus between organizations, 35
use of term, 34–35

C

C, 24, 25, 113
Caldiera, Gianluigi, 119–20
Caldwell, Bruce, 29
Canfora, G. A., 112
CAP-Netron, 7
Caruso, Joseph M., 77–83, 87–88, 89
Causality, 113
Changes in reusable software, 58
Chen, Deng-Jyi, 118–19
Chester, Rowena O., 124
Chief Software Development Manager, 92
Clancy, Michael J., 112
Classes, 49, 50
Code, measuring developed, 59
Code libraries, measuring, 45–46
Code Reuseability Analysis (CRA), 122
Commercial off-the-shelf (COTS) software, measuring, 42–43
Complete applications, 43
Complexity
    Halstead Software Science, 111–12